The Illustrated HITLER DIARY

1917-1945

Marshall Cavendish
London & Sydney

Galahad Books
New York

Edited by Stuart Laing
Designed by Graham Beehag

First edition
published and distributed by:

Marshall Cavendish Books Limited
58 Old Compton Street
London W1V 5PA

Galahad Books, a division of
A & W Publishers, Inc.
95 Madison Avenue
New York, N.Y. 10016

IN THE U.K., COMMONWEALTH AND REST
OF THE WORLD, EXCEPT NORTH AMERICA

IN THE UNITED STATES OF AMERICA

ISBN 0 85685 863 3

ISBN 0-88365-453-9
Library of Congress Number 80-66403

First printing 1980
© MARSHALL CAVENDISH LIMITED 1980
All rights reserved
Printed in Great Britain by
Redwood Burn Limited
Trowbridge & Esher

CONTENTS

Politics

Friends & enemies

War machine

Decisive battles

INTRODUCTION

ON 30 APRIL 1945 ADOLF HITLER SHOT HIMSELF, so ending the Nazi nightmare. Even the deaths of 6 million Jews, 14 million Russians and 1 in 7 of the population of Poland had formed only a part of the savagery and destruction which had engulfed Europe. Yet, only 30 years before his death in the Chancellory bunker, the man responsible for World War II had been an obscure casualty statistic of World War I. *The Illustrated Hitler Diary* is a record of the years in between, contained in the words of Hitler himself.

Hitler's formative years were spent in Vienna, where anti-semitism was a common focus for working class disaffection, and he was imbued with a philosophy of race which he never abandoned. He moved in a world of grandiose fantasy as an escape from the realities of poverty and failure. His experiences during World War I confirmed his admiration for the values of comradeship, discipline and authoritarianism. To Hitler, war was not only a crusade against bourgeois values and Marxism, but also a relief from the aimlessness of civilian life. As his power grew, an instinctive talent for rabble-rousing formed the basis of the 'Hitler myth' of invincibility. Having found a role, he was able to play it to the hilt but always retained an objective view of the political realities. This ability extended to an almost hypnotic hold over his subordinates. By ensuring that their areas of responsibility overlapped, he was always able to divide and rule – even when his judgements were manifestly wrong.

Nowhere is Hitler's character betrayed more clearly and forcefully than in the speeches, radio broadcasts, writings and conversations which form the basis of *The Illustrated Hitler Diary*. From propagandist for the insignificant German Worker's Party to ruined and defeated Fuhrer, Hitler's pronouncements display the essence of Nazism. This archive material, supported by contemporary photographs and expert analysis, provides a unique opportunity to re-examine one of the century's most sinister yet significant influences.

Politics

First principles
Political warfare
Nazi diplomacy
Nazi institutions

Hitler and Ribbentrop consolidate their
understanding with the Vatican.

FIRST PRINCIPLES

THE KEYSTONE OF THE NAZI GOSPEL was race. The whole structure of the 'New Order', its worship of combat and ruthlessness, its theory of government and its vilest cruelties were the result of a racial theory of history. The theory was not new and emphatically not the original concept of Adolf Hitler; on the contrary, elements of it had long been advocated in Germany—sometimes by the most gifted or respected figures in the arts or letters. A thoroughly racist nationalism was not confined strictly to the Germans, but it was among them that it achieved the widest acceptance and respectability.

From his schooldays Hitler was a fanatical German nationalist with a rancorous hatred of the other, mostly slavic, races which made up the Austro-Hungarian Empire. He also learned anti-semitism during the first 24 years of his life while he lived in Austria. Vienna had a large Jewish population and a violent anti-semitism was a frequently-expressed staple of working class and lower middle class Austrian politics. Hitler caught the infection and became a prey to a morbid loathing of the Jews which affected his whole outlook on life. This fierce nationalism and its corresponding intolerance of other races soon furnished Hitler with an outlook on life which was in an established German tradition derived from Fichte and Hegel, Treitschke, Nietzsche and Richard Wagner. By the time he left Vienna in 1913 Hitler was later to claim that his character was fully formed and his fundamental philosophy was already worked out.

Shortly after he left Vienna and went to live in Bavaria war broke out and he joined the German army. It was to have a dreadful impact on his convictions of racial superiority. His belief in the German race was based on the idea that it would prove victorious in any struggle against other races and particularly so in warfare. This theory never wilted during the years he spent fighting in the vast charnel house of the Western front even though most of his service was against British troops in the muddy hell of the Ypres salient. By 1917 however he was a prey to anxieties over the course of the war and, when he was wounded and returned to Germany, he began to find a racial explanation for Germany's failure to triumph.

MARCH 1917

Slackers abounded and who were they but Jews. Nearly every clerk was a Jew and nearly every Jew was a clerk. The Jew robbed the whole nation and pressed it beneath his domination.

Right: *Hitler's army identification papers, taken from an early Nazi magazine. Hitler considered active service in World War I almost as a necessary qualification for any military adviser in World War II.*

In his unbalanced view the efforts of the front line soldiers were being sabotaged by 'slackers' who had safe jobs as clerks far behind the lines. His mind was already so warped that every man who held a safe job away from the fighting appeared to him to be Jewish. Here was an explanation for failure: the Jews were not shedding their blood alongside the Germans but were, on the contrary, scheming for their defeat.

Worse was to follow the anxieties of 1917. By November of 1918 the apparently invincible German armies were beaten. To many front-line soldiers the defeat was not obvious. They could tell that they had lost a series of battles and that allied pressure upon them was severe, but, unlike the generals at headquarters, they did not realize that all their military resources were exhausted and that they were facing a vast and total defeat within a few days. To such men the news that Germany was suing for peace came like a bombshell and to none of them more than Adolf Hitler. Hitler had missed the last disastrous few weeks of fighting because he was once more in hospital having been temporarily blinded in a British gas attack and it seemed to him that the calamity had destroyed his world.

10 NOVEMBER   **1918**

I could stand the greatest villainy of the century no longer. Everything went black before my eyes. In vain had two million died. Had all this happened so that a gang of wretched criminals could lay hands on the Fatherland?

Hitler could not believe that the German race had been beaten in a straight fight so he convinced himself that it had been betrayed. It seemed to him that the traitors who had struck Germany down were the civilian government (containing a number of Jews) which had been forced to negotiate the armistice. These were the 'November criminals' he swore to bring down.

Despite the fact that Hitler's mind was the most extraordinary litter of absurd prejudices, he was an acute political observer. When he decided to turn politician after the disappointment of 1918 he already had a good idea of the sort of political movement that he wished to lead.

SEPTEMBER   **1919**

The breaking of 'interest slavery' is one of the essential premises for the foundation of a new party.

His new party would have to be a socialist party, not because he had any real time for socialist theories, but because he believed that only a mass movement of the working and lower middle classes could possibly succeed in capturing power. He recognized that socialism had an attraction for the masses he wished to recruit and he had, in any case, an antipathy for the moneyed and banking classes whom he equated with the Jews. From these roots sprang a sort of half-baked economic theory (which Hitler himself hardly believed in), and the Party title, National Socialist.

                                         1921

The National Socialist Movement will, in the future, ruthlessly prevent — if necessary by force — all meetings or lectures that are likely to distract the minds of our fellow countrymen.

Hitler believed fervently in the attraction exercised by violence on a sector of the German electorate. He felt that people liked to associate themselves with successful brutality and were wary of organizations which could not defend themselves from the sort of force that the Nazis were prepared to use. From this degrading but correct view of human nature sprang the loutish stormtroopers and the hooligan electioneering which became such a familiar part of the Nazi movement. Nor was anti-semitism neglected; not just because Hitler himself was a rabid jew-hater but because it was appealing to depressed and beaten people. The Jew could be blamed for all their woes and they could draw consolation from the spectacle of stormtroopers savaging their supposed enemies. It must not be supposed that Hitler introduced anti-semitism into the politics of Bavaria but rather that he found a considerable body of opinion in sympathy with his extremist outlook.

28 JULY   **1922**

The Jew has never founded any civilization, though he has destroyed hundreds. He must spread as a disease spreads. Already he has destroyed Russia; now it is the turn of Germany and, with his envious instinct for destruction, he seeks to disintegrate the national spirit of the Germans and to pollute their blood.

The main pitch of the Nazi creed was, as always, a fervent nationalism. It was in this that the Nazis were

Above: *Hitler (on the far left) in one of the grim dugouts on the Western Front.*

distinguished from more orthodox socialist parties and so great was their insistence on it that it completely eclipsed any pretensions to genuine socialism within the Party. Hitler's mindless cry that any super-patriot was a socialist revealed that the revolution that he was organizing was not concerned with social reform. Nazism was about making the Germans 'lords of the earth' and nothing more. At the same time there was never any respect for the ideals of democracy.

NOVEMBER 1922

We will no longer submit to a state which is built on the swindling idea of the majority. We want a dictatorship.

From the very start, Nazi philosophy condemned government by the majority and extolled the decisiveness of dictatorship. If people longed for a leader the Nazis offered to supply one in the shape of party Fuhrer Hitler.

As Germany plunged into the crisis caused by hyperinflation, Hitler made quite plain both the Nazi Party's sterility of ideas and its true purpose. The Nazis had no economic policy capable of solving Germany's problems—indeed Hitler was profoundly uninterested in economics. The Nazi answer to every challenge was that it could be overcome by an effort of will.

8 NOVEMBER 1923

I want to know neither rest nor peace until the November criminals have been overthrown, until on the ruins of the wretched Germany of today there should arise once more a Germany of power and greatness.

The sole, true purpose of the Nazi Party and, indeed, Hitler's own concern with politics was to reverse the verdict of 1918. Nazi speakers continuously made vengeful demands for the downfall of the government of 'November criminals' who had signed the humiliating Treaty of Versailles. No other aspect of government held the faintest interest for them. They considered neither economic nor social reform but were blindly determined to seize power simply to re-establish the military power of Germany. This over-riding concern led Hitler to make the abortive and slightly ludicrous 'Beer Hall Putsch' of 1924. After its failure he was arrested and tried.

Below: *Hitler, flanked by two bodyguards, reviewing a mass gathering of Brownshirts in* 1937.

FEBRUARY 1924

There is no such thing as high treason against the traitors of 1918. The day will come when these rough companies will grow to battalions, the battalions to regiments, the regiments to divisions; the old cockade will be taken from the mud, the old flags will wave again.

Above: *Hitler (far left) sits for a photograph with a group of friends during his imprisonment in the fortress at Landsberg, Bavaria. Hitler always retained a special fondness for them.*

Men do not perish as a result of lost wars but as a result of loss of that force of resistance which is continued only in pure blood. All who are not of good race in this world are chaff. The Germans are the highest species of humanity on this earth.

Hitler made it quite clear that he was unrepentant and used his trial as a forum to assure the German public that his hour would come and that his ambitions for the re-establishment of German greatness would be realized.

The short and comfortable period of imprisonment which followed Hitler's trial was time which he used to formulate his theories in his turgid book *Mein Kampf.* These theories were a haphazard jumble of ill-digested philosophies with a strongly racist core. He believed that history was determined by the struggle between races for supremacy over each other. In this world of struggle there was one race with a natural advantage over the others. This was the Aryan race which was responsible for all civilized advance and which had a natural duty to enslave lesser races such as the Slavs so that it could continue to push forward the boundaries of human achievement. For this *herrenvolk* (master race) to show pity for its inferiors or to allow them equality was as contrary to the laws of nature as a hungry lion sparing his prey. No one was quite certain who was Aryan but it was roughly calculated that the inhabitants of Ireland, Britain, France north of the Seine, the Low Countries, Scandinavia and Germany were reasonably pure specimens. Europeans south of that line were hopelessly bastardized Aryans whose blood had been polluted by Mediterranean races.

Among the acknowledged Aryan countries, the Germans were especially Aryan—although they were still not simon-pure—and all Aryans had to be careful not to interbreed with people of lesser races because only pure Aryans were the creative, forceful people capable of running the world.

In addition to all this, the Aryans had an elite and an enemy. The elite were of the Nordic race who were super-Aryans and who exhibited all the characteristics of leaders and who were probably blond, blue-eyed and ruthless. The enemy was the Jewish people—who were uncreative but maliciously determined to confound the Aryan's natural destiny (in a number of ways, including polluting his blood by seducing or raping Aryan women). The answer to all this was to unite the Aryan people (or at least the Germans) and allow them, quite naturally, to enslave the Slavs and root out the Jews.

This outlook on life coloured every aspect of living. For instance, government was on the famous *Fuhrerprinzip* (leadership principle): just as the Aryans would rise to the top in any conflict between peoples so, by a process of natural selection, strong leaders would appear in every walk of life and they would make decisions with no-holds-barred brutality—the survival and triumph of the race were more important than any individual right to life, justice or liberty.

27 FEBRUARY   **1925**

I alone lead the movement and no one can impose conditions on me.

Unfortunately for Hitler he had a certain difficulty in establishing his *Fuhrerprinzip* satisfactorily when he emerged from his incarceration. The Nazi Party in North Germany under the leadership of Gregor Strasser challenged his position. With deft political skill Hitler met the challenge and established himself and his claim to absolute power within the Party. He consolidated this principle over the succeeding years until he was quite unaccustomed to anything but fulsome flattery and fawning obedience from other Party members.

1930

Hard reality has opened the eyes of millions of Germans to the lies, swindles and betrayals of the Marxist deceivers of the people.

Hitler had long realized that Communism was competing as an ideology for the loyalty of the German working class. Despite the pseudo-socialist leanings of his own Party, he made no common cause with the Communists but treated them with outright and violent hostility.

The reason for this was not simply because they represented an opposing political party but because they were part of a Jewish conspiracy against the Aryan. Marx had been a Jew and so, according to Nazi philosophy, manifestly an intriguer against the natural law of Aryan superiority. With satanic cunning he had invented Communism which sought to beguile Germans into a spurious international brotherhood and away from achieving their destiny as a strictly national brotherhood. Hitler held that the evil Marx had destroyed Russia and that his ideas threatened to destroy his beloved Germany.

After Hitler had come to power as Chancellor of Germany in 1932 he had many years during which he achieved a series of glittering successes. Although his native shrewdness had a lot to do with his triumphs even he could not fail to see that a measure of good fortune had made some contribution.

15 MARCH   **1936**

I go the way that Providence dictates with the assurance of a sleep-walker.

27 JUNE   **1937**

When I look back on the five years which lie behind us, then I feel I am justified in saying: 'that has not been the work of man alone'.

As Hitler reflected upon his life's astonishing course from Austrian dropout to leader of a mighty nation he began to feel that he was a man of destiny—something which was to have fateful consequences in future years. He claimed that he had been marked by a divine providence as a towering historical figure. As long as he obeyed his instincts he would be successful. This theory hardened dangerously into a conviction that he could not fail and strengthened the resolution with which he ignored the advice of his subordinates. After the war, the German generals frequently complained that they had been overruled with disastrous consequences. The self-confidence with which Hitler believed that he knew better than his military advisers stemmed from his belief that he was the pet creature of Providence.

22 NOVEMBER   **1936**

Through all the centuries, force and power are the determining factors. Only force rules. Force is the first law.

In ominous warning of the excesses to come, Nazi policy was expressed with a barbarous encouragement to brutality. This partly derived from a love for decisive action and the feeling that an unshrinking ruthlessness was the mark of a leader. Indeed, the leadership of the future New Order was to be found from the ranks of those unafraid to take decisions which could cause suffering. This leadership would be essentially classless as each new generation would naturally throw up new leaders who would prove themselves in the constant struggle to keep the Aryan people in their dominant position. But the incitement to harsh measures was not only directed to the new Nazi leadership class – although it was among them that it obviously found the most willing disciples.

In Nazi philosophy, pitilessness was natural and any merciful considerations were an artificial restraint. The Aryan was a stern warrior; it was normal for him to enslave and massacre his defeated inferiors. Any play on his generous emotions was against nature and might lead to his loss of supremacy, so he must be educated to pursue his struggle against other peoples unhindered by any weak idea of clemency. Above all he must allow no pollution of his blood by lesser races.

By 1938, the aggressive policies of the Nazi state had led it towards the achievement of its first objectives. The Treaty of Versailles was virtually a dead letter as Germany was openly rearming and had militarily occupied the Rhineland. The plan to bring the whole scattered ethnic German population of Europe within the boundaries of the new Reich had also progressed. Austria had already been incorporated, and as Hitler made threats against Czechoslovakia, European statesmen were disposed to take the Nazi gospel seriously. Unfortunately, few of them made a deep analysis of Nazi intentions and they maintained a muddled idea that Nazism was simply a Pan-German nationalism. Hitler encouraged this misapprehension. He made no mention for a while of his intention to enslave other races and indeed pretended that uniting the ethnic German people was the limit of his ambitions.

27 SEPTEMBER   **1938**

We want no Czechs.

This deception was enough to bring about the fall of Czechoslovakia but when this was followed by German preparations against Poland the absolutely limitless nature of Nazi ambitions became apparent. Naturally enough, opposition to German expansion stiffened; but Hitler was blind to the causes and nature of this reaction.

30 JANUARY   **1939**

If the international Jewish financiers should again succeed in plunging the nations into a world war, the result will be the annihilation of the Jewish race throughout Europe.

To Hitler's blinkered reason it seemed clear that any opposition to the Aryan's moves to become 'lord of the earth' was fomented by 'international Jewry'. It was always the Jew who was putting obstacles in Hitler's way, conspiring to deprive the Aryan of his rightful position of superiority. Attacks upon the German Jews had already begun with the Nuremberg race laws of 1935 but, during

Above and opposite: *Graphically exaggerating the features of Jewish and Aryan races formed the central theme of Hitler's poster campaigns.*

Baut
Jugendherbergen
und Heime

Right: *One of Himmler's dedicated officers lines up Polish civilians, probably on suspicion of being Jewish. Between them, Himmler's SS and Gestapo slaughtered 2.6 million of Poland's 3 million Jews.*

1939, it became clear to those who paid close attention that a far worse and all-embracing fate would overtake any Jews who came into German clutches.

23 MAY   **1939**

Danzig is not the subject of the dispute at all. It is a question of expanding our living space in the East. Besides, the population of non-German territories will be available as a source of labour.

In private, Hitler also revealed during 1939 that his attack on Poland was not planned simply as part of a programme to unite ethnic Germany but as the beginning of an attempt to find *lebensraum* (living space) for the German people in the East. At the same time, his opinion of the Poles differed from his opinion of their western allies. The Poles were Slavs and it was axiomatic that their lands should be taken from them to provide the Germans with *lebensraum*. They would become serfs of the New Order. The French were destined for different treatment: they were at least partially Aryan. As a rival military power to Germany, the Aryan Fatherland, the French would have to be militarily smashed but they were not necessarily to be kept in a state of degrading subjection.

For the British, Hitler often evinced an unlikely admiration. Several years in the trenches opposite British units had left him with a favourable impression of their powers of resistance. His ignorance of the nature of the British Empire also led him to suppose that the British showed all the Nordic talents of leadership and ruthlessness. In a muddled way he regarded the British as his natural allies and ascribed their opposition to him to the fact that they were beguiled by international Jewry.

After the defeat of Poland and France, he could only think that the Jews prevented the British from coming to terms. The day would come, he felt, when the Germans and their British cousins would join together in opposition to the forces of Jewry. While he waited for this conclusion, Hitler busied himself with his monstrous schemes for the Slavs who had fallen into his power.

2 OCTOBER   **1940**

The Poles in direct contrast to our German workmen are especially born for hard labour. There can be no question of improvement for them. On the contrary, it is necessary to keep the standard of life low in Poland and it must not be permitted to rise. The Polish landlords must cease to exist. They must be exterminated wherever they are. There should be only one master for the Poles—the Germans. Therefore all representatives of the Polish intelligentsia are to be exterminated— such is the law of life. The lowest German workman and the lowest German peasant must always stand economically ten per cent above any Pole.

With unspeakable insensitivity, Hitler outlined plans to destroy the culture of the Poles by murdering all classes in Polish society which might have a claim to their nation's leadership. He made it clear that the enslavement of the rest of the population was not to be an easy one.

9 OCTOBER   **1940**

The other half of the Czechs must be deprived of their power, eliminated and shipped out of the country. This applies particularly to the racially mongoloid part and to the major part of the intellectual class.

Czech lands were to be turned over to Germans and the Czech population was to be exterminated or dispersed far and wide as forced labour for the German conquerors. In the end, that which had been Czechoslovakia would simply be another part of the German Reich.

In due course, Hitler's attack on Russia brought vast areas of that country within the area controlled by the Nazis. The Russians too were Slavs and they were treated in the same inhuman fashion as the other peoples of Eastern Europe. Nearly 4,000,000 Russian soldiers were taken prisoner in the early, successful part of the German campaign and a very great number of them were simply allowed to starve or freeze to death. At least

2,000,000 Russian prisoners died in German captivity and another 1,000,000 were unaccounted for. This sort of brutal treatment provoked the Russians to resist the occupying forces—something which only provoked the Nazis to a still more savage repression.

16 JULY   **1941**

The Russians have now ordered partisan warfare behind our lines. This has some advantages for us: it enables us to eradicate everyone who opposes us.

Harsh though the racial theories of the Nazis made them to the Slavs, an even more extreme approach was reserved for the Jews. In Hitler's view the Slav simply was not human and might be murdered or not to suit the Aryan's convenience, but the Jews were such a danger to the race that killing them was a positive duty enjoined on the Party faithful.

WINTER   **1941-42**

The fate of a few filthy, lousy Jews and epileptics is not worth bothering about.

The logical culmination of Nazi philosophy was reached in the systematic liquidation of the Jewish population of Europe. This genocide provides one of the blackest chapters in human history made darker by the random cruelty of its executors. Not only were millions of innocents callously destroyed but many of them were subjected to horrific torture—injection with gas gangrene or very slow asphyxiation were just two of a myriad ways in which the Nazis added to the agonies of their victims.

It is true that Hitler was not closely associated with the extermination of the Jews. He spent the last years of the war almost totally absorbed in the military problems of the Reich but there is little doubt that the holocaust was carried out at his instigation and that he kept in touch with its progress. The actual details of the mass slaughter were left to his pallid subordinate Himmler, Reichsfuhrer SS. Throughout the war, Himmler reported to Hitler in secret talks 'unter vier Augen' at which no one else was allowed to be present. The whole dreadful attempt to eliminate an entire race sprang directly from Hitler's 'discovery' during his youth in Austria that the Jews were the authors of all he hated. This consuming belief formed the bedrock of Nazi philosophy and never flickered or wavered even at the end when, during the last days in the bunker, Hitler's will finished with an exhortation to his successors to follow his racial policies.

POLITICAL WARFARE

THE WHOLE OF HITLER'S STRUGGLE for control of Germany was carried on in an unusual political environment which offered him enormous advantages. When World War I ended, the Weimar Republic was established and survived a number of coups and counter-coups from the left and the right. However, while it was a democratic government, it was unable to ensure that democracy flourished in all parts of Germany. Hitler was involved in the politics of Munich, the capital of the state of Bavaria, in which a very different regime was in power. Immediately after the war, Bavaria was established as a republic in a bloodless coup but, after a political assassination, it became a workers soviet. This soviet was savagely crushed by the regular German army (the Reichswehr) and its allies of the free-corps (unofficial bands of armed ex-soldiers and rough-necks). After this suppression of the soviet in 1919 real power in Bavaria remained with the political right and any pretence to the contrary was abandoned in March 1920 when a conservative regime was installed under Gustav von Kahr.

As a nationalist and anti-communist Hitler was, to an important extent, under the protection of the Bavarian regime. He seemed in those early days after the war to be an unimportant demagogue with the useful ability of mobilizing popular support against the left-wing. He was, of course, unreliable and he represented a sizeable threat to peace and order with his tactics of physical confrontation with the communists but, for better or worse, he enjoyed the qualified approval of the Kahr government and therefore the limited backing of the Bavarian state. This added up to a certain amount of police sympathy, tolerance from the judiciary, some secret funds provided by the Army for political purposes and a license to behave in a violent and provocative manner which would never have been tolerated in a properly conducted democracy. From this unusual situation stemmed the first of the Nazi involvements with the dirty-tricks department of politics.

AUGUST   **1921**

I made it a special point to organize a suitable defence squad. The best means of defence is attack, and the reputation of our hall-guard squads stamped us as a political fighting force and not as a debating society.

The general passion and intemperance of the Bavarian political scene made physical clashes at meetings quite common. Hitler's best known technique in argument was to scream at his opponent until the latter gave up; this stood him in good stead, as did his employment of some of Munich's sturdier citizenry to protect his meetings by battering his opponents into silence or ejecting them. The techniques of violence and intimidation formed a major part of Hitler's political campaigning. From protecting their own meetings it was a short step for the Nazis to start disrupting the rallies and speeches of other parties.

SEPTEMBER   **1921**

We got what we wanted. Ballerstedt did not speak.

This was not done simply to deny others the right of free speech but also because violence was an inherent part of the Nazi creed. Hitler believed firmly that successful employment of violence was attractive—in crude terms, it gave the Nazis the look of winners while his savaged rivals looked like losers. Yet the whole paraphernalia of violence was built upon the foundation of a biased political system. The police and judiciary of right-wing Bavaria were lenient to the Nazis and the other right-wing political parties; the leftwingers found it much harder to employ rough tactics without provoking retaliation from the authorities.

The atmosphere of Bavaria was heavily influenced by the continuing existence of the free-corps. It seems incredible today that any government could tolerate a situation in which uniformed and armed bands of politically motivated men posed a constant threat to order, but Kahr's regime was quite happy with it. The Reichswehr was the unofficial patron of the free-corps and looked upon them almost as an extension of itself (the Reichswehr had been limited to a total strength of 100,000 men by the Treaty of Versailles and many Reichswehr officers secretly regarded the free-corps as a pool of reinforcements for the day when the Treaty should be broken and the Reichswehr expanded again). Given this attitude it was not long before Hitler's Beer-hall guards were formed up as a free-corps. These men of the Stoss-trupp-Hitler and other Sturmabteilung (SA) organizations grew in numbers until they paraded 800 strong for a pitched battle with the Reds in Coburg in August 1922.

Once Hitler had an expanding force of armed men his thoughts turned to an undemocratic seizure of power.

Opposite: *Hitler's amateurish Putsch of 1923 was rewarded by a sympathetic court with only a light prison sentence.*

I can confess quite calmly that from 1919 to 1923 I thought of nothing else than a coup d'état.

Hitler had never had any time for playing any political game by the rules and he was excited by the ease with which Mussolini had succeeded in taking over Italy in a putsch. All these considerations became much more pressing as Germany's political ferment was redoubled by the dramatic events of 1923. In the autumn of 1922 the German government had confessed that it was unable to continue to make the large annual reparation for World War I. The French were unsympathetic and occupied the Ruhr—which contained 80 per cent of Germany's industry and resources. In retaliation the Germans adopted a policy of strikes and non co-operation which severely damaged their ailing economy and triggered off the collapse of their currency in the second half of 1923. On 1 July a dollar could fetch 160,000 marks but, on 1 November it was worth 130,000 million. Naturally enough this unsettled situation produced a considerable unease among the people of Germany. Hitler recognized

that the volatile atmosphere of 1923 was a transient thing and he resolved to take advantage of it.

The trouble was that the Nazi movement was not really powerful enough in 1923 to make a convincing play for power, but Hitler hoped that a brutal dispensation with legality might still see him through. The storm-troopers of the SA could be greatly swelled in numbers by alliance to the various free-corps adherents of other right-wing factions. Hitler reckoned that these rag-tag soldiers might be enough to seize power in Bavaria and, with luck, march from Munich on Berlin for his final triumph. At the beginning of November 1923 the 15,000 men of the SA were put on the alert and a suitable opportunity for the coup occurred on the 8th. On that day the three most powerful men in Bavaria—State Commissioner Kahr, local Army Commander Lossow and Police Chief Seisser were at a political meeting at the *Burgerbraukeller* where they could be handily seized by a Nazi strongarm squad.

At first all went well and armed stormtroopers kept the crowd in the *Burgerbraukeller* cowed while Hitler bundled Kahr, Lossow and Seisser into a side room. By dint of histrionic threats and the news that Field-Marshal Erich Ludendorff, the prestigious wartime military leader, was his supporter, Hitler persuaded his three captives to join him. However, when the cheers in the *Burgerbraukeller* had died away and an excited Hitler had left to monitor

the progress of the SA in taking over the city, Kahr, Lossow and Seisser changed their tack. They were right-wingers with a certain amount of sympathy for the anti-red stance of the Nazis but they were, first and foremost, conservatives. To men of their stamp, Hitler was a hooligan and rioter with a limited value as a hammer of the Communists and a frightening prospect as head of state. As soon as they were free they sped off to organize resistance to the Nazi putsch.

9 NOVEMBER   **1923**

Messrs Kahr, Lossow and Seisser could not be so foolish as to turn machineguns on the aroused people.

On the morning of 9 November the main force of the SA under command of ex-army officer Ernst Rohm was besieged in the War Ministry by regular army units summoned by Lossow. Hitler and his side-kick Hermann Goering organized a relief column of 2000-3000 of their men and, accompanied by Ludendorff as figurehead, they led it through the streets of Munich. All the evidence is that Hitler was not seeking to take on the forces of the state but hoped that the soldiers would be unwilling to fire on his men—particularly as they were led by Ludendorff. They ran into the first cordon of Seisser's police on the Ludwig Bridge but brushed them aside assisted by Goering's threats to execute some hostages that they had taken. The second police cordon on the edge of the Odeonsplatz gave them a different reception and, after a short gunfight, the Nazis ran for it leaving three policemen and 16 of their own number dead.

Hitler's first and rather bungled attempt to seize power had failed, but the Bavarian machine for political manipulation made sure that retribution was slight. By ordinary standards his offences were serious and, in more liberal democracies, the penalty would have been equally serious—but things worked differently in the Bavaria of the roaring twenties. Police and judiciary were studded with Nazis and had an overall right-wing bias. Some of them might not like Hitler but nearly all of them agreed with the nationalistic ideas that he stood for.

26 FEBRUARY   **1924**

If we committed High Treason, then countless others did the same. I deny all guilt. I feel myself the best of Germans who wanted the best for the German people.

Hitler's trial was a masterpiece of double standards in which he revelled in his admission of guilt and boasted of his objectives. There had to be some lip service to the ideas of justice and, since the accused had abducted high officials of the state, shot at the police, organized an insurrection and insisted on admitting it, he could hardly be found not guilty; but everybody knew his heart was in the right place and he was given the minimum sentence. Although this minimum was a stiff five years, Hitler only served nine months in a comfortable, open regime before he was paroled.

Although Hitler had survived the crisis without a heavy punishment he was quick to learn its lessons. He was still intent on taking power by force but he realized that a certain amount of polish could cut out the amateurish mistakes which had made for failure in 1923.

9 NOVEMBER   **1936**

We recognized that it is not enough to overthrow the old State, but that the new State must have been previously built up and be practically ready to one's hand.

Hitler was aware that his forces had not really had the remotest idea of how to seize control during the night of 8 November 1923 when they were presented with a brief opportunity, and he determined that the next time would be different. It has been said that the Nazis were less of a political party than an organized conspiracy against the state, and this became more and more obvious during the decade after the abortive Beer-hall Putsch. The Nazi Party itself was organized in a number of different departments which were parallel to the official state departments that they were to take over. Under the new system, Germany was divided up into a number of Party areas, each under a *gauleiter* or local Party leader. There were Nazi departments of economics, education and justice— plus a Hitler Youth movement, League of German maidens and Women's Union. The Nazi Party's activities stretched into every aspect of German life until it represented an alternative state ready to move into action and sequester power at its leader's call.

While Hitler was kicking his heels in prison for nine months after his trial, the Nazis progressed from their role as a local, Bavarian political force into a national party. In alliance with other nationalist parties they had taken to legitimate politics and tried their fortune at the polls. At the first attempt, their coalition won a surprising 32 seats in the Reichstag (national parliament) but this was cut to 14 in the elections of December 1924. The next few years were slow ones for the Nazis as their band-wagon seemed to stop rolling. Hitler himself took life easily with occasional periods of relaxation in the lovely scenery of the mountains; he even ran a mistress and a

Above: *Despite the failure of the 1923 Beer-hall Putsch, beer halls remained favourite places to hold Party meetings.*

fast Mercedes. The Party still had a dangerous image, but the only really illegitimate aspect of its activities was its continued use of the SA as political bully-boys. This interlude of calm had nothing to do with any renunciation of political trickery. It was simply that Hitler was not going to risk humiliation and failure once more by taking on the forces of the state—particularly the Army. Only when the guardians of the state had been coerced would Hitler move.

1930 brought the Depression, and its miseries were a tonic for the Nazis. The 1930 elections gave Hitler 107 brown-shirted deputies in the Reichstag and in the next year the epicene ruffian Rohm could put 300,000 SA men on the streets. This meant that the Nazis were the second strongest party in the Reichstag and were in a good position to take part in the wheeling and dealing which accompanied power-broking in the Weimar Republic.

There was no party with an overall majority in the Reichstag and the country was run by a series of minority governments. This was made possible only by the enormous dictatorial powers vested in the ageing president von Hindenburg, who could dissolve the Reichstag and appoint a Chancellor to form a cabinet and allow that Chancellor to govern without reference to the Reichstag by Presidential Decree. Hindenburg was 84 years old in 1931 and did not relish these powers but longed for a legitimate government with a clear majority to relieve him of his political duties.

Increasing electoral success for the Nazis made them the strongest party in the Reichstag and, although Hindenburg had a deep distrust of Hitler, other right-wing politicians wooed them for support. By January of 1933 practically all other options had been exhausted and Hindenburg's advisers persuaded him that, if he made Hitler Chancellor under certain strict controls, the Nazis would be unable to smash the constitution and make him a dictator.

Hindenburg's idea was to establish a majority government, at last, by effecting a coalition between the Nazis and certain other parties but to restrain their totalitarian tendencies with certain other government appointments. Hitler knew that his hour had come and that, although he had no majority in the Reichstag, his dirty tricks department could soon fix the government and the constitution and give him untrammelled power.

Opposite: *An early SS street parade, drumming up support and promoting the Nazi image of a strong Party.*
Below: *Bowing obsequiously, Hitler greets the ageing Hindenburg as Germany's new Chancellor.*

The reactionary forces believe they have me on the lead. But we shall not wait for them to act. Our great opportunity lies in acting before they do. We have no scruples, no bourgeois hesitations. They regard me as an uneducated barbarian. Yes we are barbarians. We want to be barbarians. It is an honourable title.

Opposite and above: *Two symbols of the fatal appointment of Hitler as head of state.*

On the face of it, the Nazis seemed pinned down by the terms of their coalition with the Nationalist Party and the concessions they had made to allay Hindenburg's fears. True, Hitler was made Chancellor on 30 January 1933 but the vice-Chancellor von Papen was a politician who especially enjoyed Hindenburg's trust and had been given unusual powers: he had the right to be present on all occasions when the Chancellor reported to the President and he was Minister-President of the state of Prussia. With a population of 38,000,000, Prussia was of far greater importance than the other 16 states of Germany put together, and the wily Papen calculated that its Minister-President would wield the real power in the country; but he failed to see the importance of Goering's position as Prussian Minister of the Interior with control over the police and justice departments. Only three out of the 11 cabinet posts were given to Nazis and Hitler was enjoined by the President to try and draw the Centre Party into his coalition which would give him an actual majority but tie him down further.

Hitler quickly shattered this cosy set-up by claiming, untruthfully, that the Centre Party refused to join his coalition and announcing that the Nazis would seek an overall majority in a new election.

20 FEBRUARY  1933

Now we stand before the last election. One way or the other, if the election does not decide, the decision must be brought about by other means.

In this election the gloves at last came off. As Chancellor, Hitler had the resources of the state to promote his cause—although the most effective campaigning was done by undemocratic means. Goering sacked all but Nazi sympathisers from the Prussian police and called up 25,000 SA and 15,000 SS men as 'police auxiliaries' to make absolutely sure that free speech was dead. In the rest of Germany the SA went on an orgy of intimidation and there was already a hint of a bloodbath in the air when on 27 February the Reichstag was burned to the ground.

There were some mysteries about the Reichstag blaze. It was started by the Dutch ex-communist van der Lubbe but it was so convenient for the Nazis that they have always been suspected of complicity. Whatever the truth behind it, it was undeniable that Hitler soon knew how to make good use of it.

27

28 FEBRUARY   **1933**

Restrictions on personal liberty, on the right of free expression of opinion, on the rights of assembly and association ... are permissible beyond the legal limits otherwise prescribed.

The day after the fire, he was claiming that it was all part of a Communist plot and suspending individual liberties. The election was then conducted in the most threatening manner. On 3 March Goering assured a Frankfurt audience 'I don't have to worry about justice, my mission is only to destroy and exterminate, nothing else'. On the same day, Hitler was busy bending the law so that he could deal 'legally' with any opponents.

To their eternal credit, the German people still did not give Hitler a majority in the elections which took place in the first week of March. By then the Nazis were beyond any constitutional refinement and any Communist and Social Democrat deputies who turned up for duty at the Kroll Opera House which replaced the razed Reichstag were simply arrested. Once they were out of the way the Nazis and their allies had the necessary two thirds majority to effect major constitutional change. Only one thing still commanded Hitler's respect—the German Army and its probable loyalty to President Hindenburg. Before opening the new Reichstag session he laid on a service in the garrison church at Potsdam—shrine of the old Prussian Army—which was attended by the brown-shirt Nazi deputies and high ranking officers of the Kaiser's regime in a show of continuity between the old and new nationalist ideals. As a climax to this display Hitler made an obsequious tribute to Hindenburg to keep the old soldier content and then sped back to Berlin to start the business of dealing with lesser opponents.

On 23 March the surviving deputies to the Reichstag were due to attend the Kroll Opera House to sanction an Enabling Bill to give Hitler supreme, untrammelled power. To make sure that all the deputies had a rough grasp of the way they were expected to vote, the building was surrounded and packed inside and out with ranks of SA and SS who kept up a menacing chant demanding blood if the Bill did not go through.

23 MARCH   **1933**

Germany will be free, but not through the Social Democrats. Do not mistake us for bourgeois. The star of Germany is in the ascendant, yours is about to disappear; your death-knell has sounded.

With amazing courage, Otto Wels, leader of the Social Democratic Party, rose to oppose the Bill although he was alone and defenceless and the baying of the stormtroopers could be clearly heard in the chamber. The last pretences were abandoned. Hitler leapt to his feet and screamed at Wels that his death-knell had sounded; the Bill was then hurriedly passed by an enormous majority. From that moment on Germany was a dictatorship.

There were a few centres of power which the Nazis had not yet carried and Hitler hardly paused before he moved to deal with them. The trade unions were almost the first to find that the combination of violence and sordid trickery was too much for them. Their leaders were invited to an immense workers' rally in Berlin on May Day where they listened to a reassuring speech from Hitler. While they were away the SA broke into their offices and looted them. When the union leaders returned they were beaten up and herded into concentration camps. All workers were then made members of the Nazi organized German Workers Front which banned collective bargaining.

The political parties were the next victims. Their offices were occupied one by one and their assets confiscated. On 14 July, the Nazi Party was made the only legal party in Germany. The non-Nazi members of the cabinet were sacked and replaced by Party members. After this the only sources of independence were the German states. The various state Presidents had considerable powers with control over police and appointments to the judiciary. This did not suit Hitler's book at all and Nazis were soon appointed to control the states and appoint the Party faithful to all positions of power. With the destruction of the independence of the states nearly every possible centre of resistance was gone. Hitler had not just absolute power but absolute control over every part of Germany save, perhaps, the Army.

23 SEPTEMBER   **1933**

If, in the days of our revolution, the Army had not stood on our side, then we should not be standing here today.

For a while Hitler preserved a misleading attitude of respect for the Army and a false gratitude for its restraint in not preventing his seizure of power. The time would come, however, when the Army itself would come under Nazi pressure, and it was to remain the object of the new dictator's suspicion until his death.

Opposite: 1 *September* 1939, *Hitler announces to the Reichstag the pretexts for the invasion of Poland. This sealed his grip on Germany, as the Fatherland and most of the rest of the World faced five years of war.*

NAZI DIPLOMACY

ALTHOUGH HITLER ACHIEVED STAGGERING SUCCESSES through diplomacy, it was not because he had any claims to statesmanship. His standard techniques of lying and threatening were so outlandish that it is a matter for astonishment that he pulled off coup after coup before dragging Germany and the world into the most destructive conflict in history. The truth is that he could have achieved nothing without the weakness and incompetence of his opponents.

If a graph was made showing the pace and scale of Hitler's military adventures, from his rearmament of Germany to his assault on Russia, it would represent a steeply rising curve as the interval between each advance became shorter, the violence employed became greater and its objectives ever more daring.

18 OCTOBER   **1933**

It is intolerable for us as a nation of 65 millions that we should repeatedly be dishonoured and humiliated. We will put up with no more of this.

His ambitions seemed to begin humbly enough. He had made no secret of the fact that he had never accepted the verdict of World War I or the humiliating terms imposed on Germany by the Treaty of Versailles in 1918. The terms of the Treaty that were particularly odious to him were those which limited the German armed forces to 100,000 men and banned the existence of any German air forces. However, when Hitler came to power in March 1933, a simple abrogation of the Treaty was a risky business. The French had lost 2,000,000 dead in World War I and appeared to be vengefully determined to prevent Germany from ever becoming a military threat again. When Germany had failed to make the impossibly large financial reparations demanded by the French, in compensation for war damage, in 1922, the French army simply occupied the Ruhr—which brought about the collapse of the German currency. Any attempt by Hitler to build up his armed forces in defiance of the Treaty terms could obviously be immediately thwarted by French military action. The newly acclaimed Fuhrer would need a certain guile.

To avoid a violent French reaction, the rearmament programme was begun in secret. There were limits to the extent to which German military strength could be built up before the process became known to the French and British, so Hitler determined on a diplomatic initiative to establish once and for all Germany's right to have arms.

In his rise to power he had often screamed out the frantic boast in his speeches '*Wir wollen wieder Waffen!*' ('We will have arms again'). To achieve this object he began with the mildest appeals to fairness from his opponents. He knew that many governments, and particularly the British, disapproved of the peremptory manner in which the French had disciplined Germany in 1922 and he concentrated on wheedling sympathy from the British for their beaten enemy.

Hitler's propaganda worked. Despite their overwhelming military strength the French were still war-weary and politically troubled. Criticism of their action in 1922 had affected their sense of moral certainty and, by the 1930s, they were unwilling to make any move to check Germany without British support. The British, for their part, were incredibly slow and unwilling to see the threat from Germany. When, on 16 March 1935, the German government announced its plans to re-introduce conscription and build up a peacetime army of 35 divisions with a numerical strength of 550,000 men there was a general anguish and wringing of hands among the nations of Europe but no action. Germany's decision was condemned but that was to prove no restraint upon her leader's simple determination to construct a matchless war machine.

This first success, and the accompanying glimpse of the weakness and credulity of his enemies, increased Hitler's boldness and speeded his ambitions. He could not wait for the army which he had called into being by the announcement of 16 March 1935 to be ready before he took his next gamble. It had been another specification of the hated Treaty of Versailles that the Rhineland should be demilitarized—that is to say that it should be unoccupied by troops or military installations. Hitler burned to send troops marching back into the Rhineland both in order to assert that it was an indivisible part of his new Germany and to show his contempt for the Treaty. His chance came in February 1936 when the nervous French ratified a treaty with the Soviet Union—a power which Hitler claimed, at the time, was particularly detestable to his Nazi state because it was Asiatic and Bolshevik. In response to this 'threat', German troops marched into the Rhineland on the morning of 7 March; that evening, the Fuhrer made a gloating speech in the packed Reichstag.

The occupation of the Rhineland had been an enormous risk which only a man as possessed as Hitler would have taken. The German army had only mustered one division to make the march into the Rhineland and, of that, only three battalions had crossed the Rhine. If the worst had come to the worst these puny forces could only have been strengthened by a few brigades, while the French with their Polish and Czech allies could have immediately mobilized 90 divisions and brought up reserves of 100 more. To make the situation even more dangerous, the re-occupation of the Rhineland was not a mundane breach of the Treaty of Versailles but a *casus foederis*— that is to say that it virtually obliged France to declare war. However, despite the terrifying prospect of a humiliating climb-down, Hitler was confident that the French would make no move against him, and he was right.

After this success, Hitler's diplomacy began to take on a new edge. His scorn for his weak and divided opponents and his growing confidence in the military strength that he was building up led him to make ever more unreasonable demands and to couple them with threats. There were now fewer references to the peaceful intent of his government in his strident blusterings in the Reichstag and Sportpalast.

21 NOVEMBER   **1937**

What the world shuts its ears to today it will not be able to ignore in a year's time.

5 NOVEMBER   **1937**

Germany's problem can only be resolved by means of force.

All this time, every propaganda vehicle in his new Reich was striving to give the impression that Germany commanded incomparable dynamism and unstoppable force. The September rally at Nuremberg in 1936 lasted one whole exhausting week as the Nazi leaders ranted to vast crowds and hundreds of thousands of men paraded. The huge stadium, the repeated baying of '*Sieg Heil*' by the crowd, the smoking torches, the massed bands and the perfect goose-stepping by rank upon rank of armed men made a terrifying impression on observers.

Below: *Hitler leads a procession of Nazi dignitaries at one of the pre-war Nuremberg rallies. These mass gatherings were staged as much for the benefit of international observers as for the Party faithful, and played their part in producing the policy of appeasement followed by the Western powers.*

The whole history of Austria is just one uninterrupted act of High Treason. I am absolutely determined to make an end of all this. The German Reich is one of the great powers and nobody will raise his voice if it settles its border problems.

It soon became transparent that Hitler's next move would be against Austria but, on this occasion, he would have to reckon with more than the feeble resolve of Britain and France. Austria was under the protection of Fascist Italy which seemed as concerned as Germany with military adventure. However, Hitler had long been convinced that Germany's only practicable allies were Italy or Great Britain. While the British showed no signs of wanting any alliance with Germany, and as his contempt for them grew with every demonstration of their government's weakness, he began to woo Italy and its Duce Mussolini.

Mussolini agreed to visit Germany. On 23 September 1937 Hitler received him at Munich in front of a monster parade of the SS. The rest of the visit was calculated to overawe the Italian leader who attended the army manoeuvres, saw the Krupp armament factories at Essen and watched Hitler address a crowd of 800,000. When he left he was determined never to oppose the new Germany and, although he was not always eager for a strict military alliance with Germany over the succeeding years, he was, to all intents and purposes, in the Nazi camp. In return, Hitler lavished a quite unjustifiable loyalty and affection upon his pretentious, ineffective new ally.

If other measures prove unsuccessful, I intend to invade Austria with armed forces. The whole operation will be directed by myself.

I will never forget, whatever may happen, if he (the Duce) should ever need any help or be in any danger, he can be convinced that I shall stick to him, whatever may happen, even if the whole world were against him.

Top: *Hitler needed Mussolini's consent for his plans to annexe Austria—then under Italy's protection.*
Above: *The view the British press took of the two leaders' relationship.*
Opposite: *Chamberlain's gullibility and terror of another war was all the encouragement Hitler needed.*

At the beginning of 1938 Hitler began to make the threatening, abusive overtures to Austria which he regarded as the diplomatic preliminaries to the forcible reunification of her German-speaking people with his Third Reich. Every utterance grew more unrestrained and on 12 February he summoned the Austrian Chancellor to demand that Austrian Nazis should be given virtual control of his government. When the wretched Chancellor managed to escape back to his own country, he tried to organize a plebiscite of the Austrian people that would prove once and for all that they were opposed to the Nazis, and that they rejected Hitler's claim that they were willing to be incorporated in the Reich. Hitler always favoured violent solutions and had, in any case, been veering towards an outright invasion of Austria. News of the plebiscite made up the Fuhrer's mind for him. On 11 March Austrian Nazis took to the streets and those Nazis in government appealed to Hitler to restore order. That night Mussolini indicated that he would not interfere to save Austria and, at daybreak on the 12th, the tanks and trucks rumbled over the frontier.

For me this is the proudest hour of my life.

Militarily the take-over of Austria was bloodless. Although Hitler enjoyed a triumphal entry into Vienna, he did not find his success absolutely satisfying. It was military victory he craved and not just diplomatic success. When the German people ratified his Austrian success in the usual rigged elections to the Reichstag (99.08 per cent of the votes of Austrians and Germans approved his actions), he seemed to have ascended a new pinnacle of achievement. That was on 10 April but, before the end of

Below: *Another triumph for Hitler's special brand of international diplomacy as German troops are welcomed in Saltzburg.*

May, the restless desire for new adventures led him to initiate threats against Czechoslovakia.

20 MAY   **1938**

It is not my intention to smash Czechoslovakia by military action in the immediate future without provocation, unless an unavoidable development of political conditions inside Czechoslovakia forces the issue, or political events in Europe create a particularly favourable opportunity which may never recur.

Below: *Hitler meets with the Czech War Minister to press his demand for the cession of the Sudetenland.*

30 MAY   **1938**

It is my unalterable decision to smash Czechoslovakia by military action in the near future.

Here the risk of war with the Western powers was considerably greater. Czechoslovakia was a democracy and the Czechs were demonstrably not German, while Austria had been a clerical fascist state with a Germanic population—Hitler himself was Austrian. Sentiment in the British and French democracies was obviously pro-Czech and Czechoslovakia itself was a well-armed and doughty partner in a French alliance purposely designed to hold Germany in check. For a while Hitler vacillated between fear of a general war if he attacked Czechoslovakia and a reckless disregard for any of the consequences of his actions.

18 JUNE   **1938**

There is no danger of a preventive war against Germany. I will decide to take action against Czechoslovakia only if I am convinced that France will not march and therefore England will not intervene.

27 SEPTEMBER   **1938**

If France and England strike, let them do so. It's a matter of complete indifference to me. Today is Tuesday; by next Monday we shall be at war.

Hitler's initial claim was for the Sudetenland which fringed the borders of Czechoslovakia and which contained a majority of ethnic Germans. The Sudetenland Nazis were instructed to provoke the Czech authorities. Once suppressed, Hitler then threatened the Czechs with retribution and demanded the cession of the Sudetenland to the Reich. The Czechs met these threats with calm determination for they were confident in their military strength and the alliance with France. Just as the outbreak of general war seemed inevitable, the humiliation of the West was ensured by the personal intervention of the British Prime Minister, Neville Chamberlain. In a series of meetings with the Fuhrer, Chamberlain was misguided enough to believe his assertion that the Sudetenland was the last territorial claim Germany had to make in Europe. He was, however, shrewd enough to realize that Hitler would plunge the continent into war if his claims were denied. Desperate to avoid this, Chamberlain and the French government put enormous pressure on the Czechs to accept dismemberment by Germany. Deserted by their allies the Czechs had to acquiesce as the Germans marched into the Sudetenland on 1 October and the Czech President was forced into exile.

It was clear to me from the first moment that I could not be satisfied with the Sudeten territory. That was only a partial solution.

Yet again Hitler's triumph did not seem complete to him. He had the Sudetenland but he hankered after a conqueror's entry into the Czech capital of Prague. The loss of the fortifications in the Sudetenland and of various territories to Poland and Hungary, who had played the jackal to Hitler's lion, had rendered the once formidable Czech state helpless. Hitler was beyond any conception of restraint and, on 14 March 1939, Hacha, the elderly new Czech President, was ushered into the Fuhrer's presence. When Goering threatened to order the bombing of Prague Hacha fainted. When he had been brought round he was forced to sign a communique placing 'the fate of the Czech people in the hands of the Fuhrer'. Two hours later German troops crossed the frontier. On the 15th Hitler had his entry into Prague.

Below: *The Duke of Windsor believed he could help in avoiding war between England and Germany.*

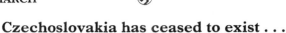
Czechoslovakia has ceased to exist . . .

This latest of Hitler's diplomatic coups finally hardened the British against him. He was not to know it but he had reached the end of the line with the British government. A disillusioned Chamberlain quickly extended a guarantee to Poland of her territorial integrity. The French only needed a British lead and soon followed suit. Any attack on Poland now meant a war in the West but Hitler had gained so many easy successes by threats that he did not understand this. One by one the dominoes had fallen and Poland was next on the list. Why should it be any different?

Should Poland adopt a threatening attitude towards the Reich, we may be driven to a final settlement, notwithstanding the existing pact with Poland.

19 APRIL   **1939**

Well, if England wants war she can have it. It will not be an easy war as they like to think, nor a war fought in the way the last one was. It will be a war of such destructiveness as no one has imagined. How can the English imagine what a modern war will be like when they are incapable of putting two fully equipped divisions in the field?

Partly to convince himself, partly to convince the German people, Hitler began a continuous series of assertions that Germany was prepared to take on all comers and particularly the British. In fact, at a time when general war had looked probable during the Czechoslovak crisis, the German public had given convincing demonstrations of their unwillingness to take on anyone and most especially the British and their allies the French. By publicly proclaiming his readiness for war and his carelessness of any consequences, the Fuhrer hoped to frighten the Western allies into further appeasement of his designs but, in effect, he was driving himself into a position from which any climbdown was unthinkable. At the same time, his threats against the Poles drove the British to make their support for Poland ever more absolute. Once the diplomatic technique of threat and bluster had run out of mileage, it not only failed to deter opponents but it even hardened their resolve. From then on Hitler's rather individual method of negotiating was plunging the world towards war.

There were certain reasons why Hitler could keep up the pressure on Poland. Treaties imposed by the victors after World War I gave Poland rights over a corridor of territory to the sea and the port of Danzig. In these areas there was a German population who could be relied on to provoke the Polish authorities. At the same time, the Poles could be falsely accused of committing atrocities on their ethnic Germans. All this tested Polish determination to resist Nazi demands for Danzig but it soon became clear that they were going to fight for their rights. This suited Hitler in every way. He had not constructed dive-bombers and Panzer divisions so that they should rust away from disuse, and the bloodless solution of the Czech crisis had not suited a man who gloried in violence and extolled ruthlessness. However, although the Poles represented the sort of target that the new German army could cut its teeth on, there remained the spectre of the British and French and the nightmare prospect of a war on two fronts should the Russians join the allies.

20 AUGUST   **1939**

In my opinion it is desirable, in view of the intentions of the two states (Germany and the Soviet Union) to enter into a new relationship and not to lose any time.

In a sudden *volte face* Hitler changed his attitude towards Russia. As subhumans the Russians had been marked down for destruction in Nazi ideology but, in the threatening circumstances of 1939, Hitler sought their alliance. By a brilliant stroke of diplomacy and luck the Germans managed to conclude a Non-Aggression pact with Russia on 24 August. Freed from the worry of Russian intervention an exultant Hitler was able to proceed with his onslaught on Poland with confidence. If the worst came to the worst he felt that he could deal with the Western allies and his orders were given. On 1 September the *Blitzkrieg* fell on Poland. Loyal to their pact, the British and French mobilized but could do nothing to save their ally. When Poland had been destroyed Hitler offered the allies peace if they accepted his conquest. Their refusal was a foregone conclusion as was Hitler's intention to turn his armed might on them.

6 OCTOBER   1939

I believe even today that there can only be real peace in Europe and throughout the World if Germany and England come to an understanding.

9 OCTOBER   1939

This does not alter the war aim. That is and remains the destruction of our enemies.

As the war spread and the conqueror overran almost the whole of mainland Europe, the time for diplomacy was past. There were small tasks with which the Fuhrer hardly bothered himself—the regulation of the Italian sphere of influence, attempts to ally with Spain, the resolution of differences between Hungary and Rumania. It was not until 1941 that the first significant reverses to Nazi arms forced Hitler's attention back to diplomacy.

5 MARCH   1941

It must be the aim of the collaboration based on the Three-Power Pact to induce Japan as soon as possible to take active measures in the Far East. Strong British forces will thereby be tied down and the centre of gravity of the interests of the United States will be diverted to the Pacific.

It had long been axiomatic to Hitler that the Americans would be dealt with 'severely' when he came to grips with them, but he was anxious to avoid this trial of strength until he had disposed of the British and the Russians. Unfortunately, American armaments were supporting the British, and the Russians were displaying great powers of resistance. Japan seemed the answer to Hitler's problems.

26 AUGUST   1941

I am convinced that Japan will carry out the attack on Vladivostock as soon as forces have been assembled. The present aloofness can be explained by the fact that the assembling of forces is to be accomplished undisturbed and the attack is to come as a surprise.

The Japanese could attack Russia in the East and, with their naval strength, frighten the Americans into abandoning Britain. With these ends in mind the Japanese were assiduously cultivated even to the extent of giving a fatal assurance that Germany would join in if friction between the Japanese and Americans erupted into war. So self-absorbed had Hitler become that it never occurred to him that the Japanese would attack America but leave Russia unmolested. Indeed, so wary was Hitler of taking on the United States before he was ready that he was prepared to accept considerable American provocation without reaction. The Japanese alliance brought Hitler the worst possible result when Japan attacked the American fleet at Pearl Harbour on 7 December 1941. His ties to Japan forced him to declare war on the United States—however, despite this disaster, the brutal treachery of the Japanese act excited his admiration. They had struck first and without warning—it was as if they had learnt diplomacy from him.

11 DECEMBER   1941

We will always strike first. We will always deliver the first blow.

Opposite: *Hundreds of members of one of Hitler's favourite institutions, the Hitler Youth, trumpet an opening fanfare at one of the Nuremberg rallies. Many were effectively fledgling recruits for the SS. The leaders of the movement promoted the Nazi gospel with a dedication designed to mobilize the whole of Germany's youth, and to instil it with a sense of mission and duty.*

NAZI INSTITUTIONS

THE NAZI STATE WAS NOT THE PARAGON of decisiveness and efficiency which Hitler promised. The reason for this was that Hitler maintained his dictatorship by a system of divide and rule which relied at first on a duplication of offices. He was an innately suspicious man and he was always happy to maintain a little friction between the great Party satraps who occupied the level of power just below his own. This purpose was achieved where he allowed interests to conflict: to make Frick Minister for the Interior and Himmler a powerful police chief ensured the certainty of struggle between them for power; economic chaos was built by making Schacht 'Plenipotentiary for War Economy' and then appointing Goering 'Delegate for the Four Year Plan'. The Foreign Service was perhaps the ultimate example of this control by division when the Minister, Neurath, had to contend with both Rosenberg, Head of the Foreign Affairs Department, and the ex-champagne-salesman Ribbentrop of the 'Ribbentrop Bureau'. Hitler was bored by the details of government and he maintained an ideal aloof-ness from the struggle as his henchmen sought to create and carve out their own institutions of power.

This competition was not conducive to good government but it did give Hitler one great advantage. It maintained his personal position of total authority. He was the source of all power. When he put the Gestapo above the law it increased the control of Gestapo-boss Himmler and levelled the area within the aegis of Frank, Commissioner of Justice and Reich Law Leader. So, the power of each of Hitler's lieutenants depended to a very real extent on his appetite for it and his ability to gain the Fuhrer's favour. A man like Robert Ley, the alcoholic leader of the Labour Front, was content simply to keep the workers' noses to the grindstone and to live fatly off graft and speculation. A man like Himmler, eventually Reichsfuhrer SS, could begin as a minor leader of a special section of Stormtroops and allow his ravening ambition to carry him to the terrifying heights which made him the most execrated man in Europe.

It was Himmler's ceaseless striving for power which

produced the most important Nazi institutions. Other parts of the ramshackle empire waxed and waned: the Ministry for the Eastern Territories, the Commission for the Ukraine, the Governor-Generalship of Poland to mention only a few of the positions of real power which proliferated in the wake of Nazi conquest. In this burrowing, amorphous mass of ill-defined fiefs, Himmler provided Hitler with a universal means to back up his authority. He created the Fuhrer's private army and police—the state within a state—which watched and disciplined the multi-tiered shambles which was the Third Reich.

Years later, as he revelled in the use of these forces so suited to his needs, Hitler tended to boast and believe that they were his own invention. To some extent he was right: he had always placed a high value on personal loyalty and his whole philosophy depended on belief in the existence of an elite; but, although the creation of the SS was his idea it would never have achieved success without Himmler and never found its alliance with the Gestapo and its *Sicherheitsdienst* (SD).

The first SS units were indeed Hitler's personal bodyguard provided by the *Stosstruppe Adolf Hitler* which was, supposedly, the elite section of the early SA. The infamous initials SS, which appeared in runic form on their distinguishing black uniforms, stood for *Schutzstaffel*. Their exceptional discipline and devotion was intended to bring Hitler control over the vastly more numerous but unreliable brownshirted SA (*Sturmabteilung*). This hope was at first unrealized. The SS distinguished themselves by failure as a party police when the Berlin SA mutinied in September 1930 and April 1931. On both occasions the civil police had to be summoned to clear the rebels out of the headquarters of Goebbels, *gauleiter* of Berlin. Although Himmler had been appointed Reichsfuhrer SS in 1929, these failures could hardly be blamed on him; he had very little authority in the Berlin area at the time, and was concentrating on building up the Munich SS with the most ferocious discipline. To check the SA, Hitler summoned the tough Ernst Rohm back from South America and made him its commander—placing him over Himmler and the discredited SS.

Chafing at this, Himmler began to burrow away for the fall of Rohm and the destruction of the SA. He was enormously reinforced for this task by the support of Reinhard Heydrich who built up the *Sicherheitsdienst* (SD) the Information Department of the SS which was an organization for terrorising Jews and Freemasons but which evolved a secret-police function. At the same time, Himmler formed an alliance with Goering against Rohm; and Goering had built up the old Prussian political police into the Gestapo (*Geheime Staatspolizei*). On 20 April 1934 Goering handed over the Gestapo to Himmler who then had control of picked troops (SS), political police (Gestapo) and secret police (SD).

Opposite: *A poster announces the holding of yet another of the famous Hitler Youth marches.*

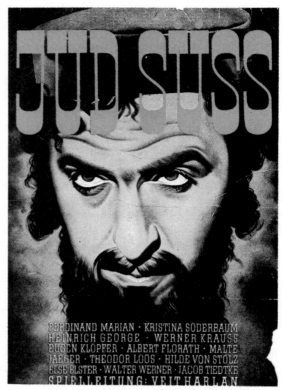

Two examples of the work of Hitler's propaganda machine: a poster for the nauseating film Jew Suss *(top) and another (above) issuing from the Nazi belief that cultural beauty lay in such images as the ideal SS man.*

Through Rohm and his companions I have enough lice under my skin. If Goering thinks that he can involve me with Himmler and Heydrich, he is mistaken.

Hitler's attitude recorded in March was not in favour of this amalgamation of power. He was already wary of Rohm's power and did not wish the Himmler-Heydrich axis to become too exalted. However, he let it pass and would, one day, be grateful for the black-uniformed departments which would be the executive power of his personal rule.

Accounts with Rohm and the SA were satisfactorily settled in the 'Night of the Long Knives' on 30 June 1934. Rohm and many other SA leaders were despatched at Hitler's orders by SS executioners. In a few days, the turbulent, 3,000,000-strong SA was deprived of menace and turned into something which was little more than a sports association. It was brought forcibly home to the Fuhrer that he owed a great deal to the comparative handful of SS who had provided him with the essential support to destroy his powerful rivals—the blackshirt organization began to enjoy more of his confidence and approval.

With the demise of the SA the last of the important institutions which had brought Hitler to power was deprived of all relevance. It joined the Reichstag and the Nazi Party itself as an organization without an executive function. The Reichstag's last effective act had been to pass the Enabling Act which gave Hitler power. After that it was only reassembled for the ritual of renewing the Act and for its packed ranks of toadies to listen to one of Hitler's speeches. None of them ever had the presumption to make a speech himself after March 1933. As for the Nazi Party, it still existed, with the rather seedy pack of *gauleiters* exerting a local and unimportant role which seems, to a jaundiced eye, to have consisted chiefly in organizing graft and corruption. There were, to be sure, many busy Nazis working hard at tasks set them by their Fuhrer but his will was backed and, where necessary, enforced by the Gestapo and the SD which kept their eyes on all the many officers of the regime.

But while the police departments of Himmler's empire burgeoned and flourished, the SS languished as a military force. Having destroyed the SA, Hitler had no wish to put the SS in its place. He wanted a political force and was in no mood to tolerate another group of Party leaders playing at soldiers when he had the German Army itself at his disposal. To some extent, Himmler himself restricted the growth of the SS, in terms of numbers, because he was insistent that it should recruit only from an elite

prescribed by his own uniquely cranky racial standards; but the idea of building a private army attracted him. In 1935, when Hitler authorized military training for the SS, there were only a few battalions of *Verfugungstruppen* who were to become the basis of the *Waffen* or armed fighting SS. There were also a few thousand *Totenkopfverbande* or Death's Head Guards whose duty was to run the concentration camps and who also provided soldiers. Hitler did not envisage the huge numbers of *Waffen SS*— comprising many army corps—which were forced upon him during the war.

The greater German Reich in its final form will include within its frontiers national entities which are not well disposed towards the German Reich. It is therefore necessary to maintain a State Military Police capable of imposing the authority of the Reich in any situation. This task can only be carried out by a State Police which has within its ranks men of the best German blood and which identifies itself with the ideology of the greater German Reich. Such a formation —proud of its racial purity—will never fraternize with the underworld which undermines the fundamental idea. Once they have proved themselves in the field, the units of the Waffen SS will possess the authority to execute their tasks as State Police.

Hitler wanted the SS to be the Party's military police, not its private army, and he wanted them under his personal control without responsibility to the Army or any other organization.

Meanwhile, Himmler and Heydrich enjoyed their police work. Heydrich had a malicious love of terrifying all and sundry and, at one time, there was hardly a single senior Nazi (probably including Himmler) who did not believe that Heydrich intended to murder him. This generated an uncomradely atmosphere which kept the most powerful satrap in line. The chief purpose of political police work at this time seemed to be to find or fabricate incriminating evidence about possible rivals or enemies. The Gestapo certainly played a role in the rather murky affair in 1938 which destroyed the German Army's two most senior generals. One was gulled into marrying a prostitute and then forced to resign by the dishonour. The other was disgraced by entirely false charges of homosexuality.

At the outbreak of war the *Waffen SS* began to come

into its own. This was in part due to the most rigorous training which soldiers of any nation can have been asked to endure. The classical Roman Army, the clockwork guards from Prussian Potsdam, the US Marines, the French Foreign Legion or the British Guards punch-drunk from the agonies of Caterham could count themselves tenderly used beside the young zealots of the SS. Yet the hefty casualty list of the SS training school at Bad Tolz lessened the terrors of actual campaigning, and *Waffen SS* units gave ample proof of their extraordinary courage and devotion in the campaigns against Poland and France. There was, however, a darker side to their fanaticism. They displayed an hysteria to prove themselves, and they took unnecessarily heavy casualties forcing the La Bassee canal against stout but doomed British resistance: in a famous incident, a froth-mouthed SS lieutenant had the helpless British survivors of the defence mown down after their surrender. It was probably not the first major *Waffen SS* atrocity and it was certainly not the last.

Hitler was pleased by the flashy way the tiny force of *Waffen SS* (two motorized divisions and an armoured regiment out of a total of 89 divisions involved) had seized the headlines in the victorious campaign in the West. He was still not prepared to take them seriously as soldiers, but he felt that they had won their spurs. In his euphoric mood of August 1940 he felt that he would soon be able to run down the size of his forces and then the SS would be able to revert to their police function as a sort of racially indoctrinated *gendarmerie*. When this happened they would be able to point to their splendid record in action.

Why Hitler was so determined on a police role for the *Waffen SS* is something of a mystery when so many of its sister organizations were already fully engaged in every sort of police work. As early as 1937, Himmler had been busily increasing the number of the Death's Head battalions to guard his proliferating concentration camps. Heydrich had grouped thousands of assorted roughs, crooks, bureaucrats, stoolpigeons, cranks and policemen in his *Reichssicherheitshauptampt* (RSHA) or Reich Main Security Office. The main elements in this umbrella organization were the Gestapo, SD and the Kripo or criminal police, but it also sheltered 'ideological research' (charged with the task of working out lunatic racial theories) and a legal department, foreign department and personnel department. From this seething hive Heydrich could produce the secret service men who served in Nazi embassies abroad or the Gestapo men who hunted for dissidents at home.

These SS and security organizations had begun the reign of terror which hailed the arrival of the New Order in Poland in 1939. The mass executions and deportations which followed Nazi conquest in the East were run or instigated by the SS. From this moment on they were the executive arm of the nightmare regime which Hitler intended to establish among the Slavs, and which was to make them the most subject people in history.

13 MARCH   **1941**

In the area of operations, the Reichsfuhrer SS is entrusted on behalf of the Fuhrer with special tasks for the preparation of the political administration, tasks which result from the struggle which has to be carried out between two opposing political systems. Within the limits of these tasks, the Reichsfuhrer SS will act independently and under his own responsibility.

He recognized this when he deliberately assigned to Himmler the task of running the areas which would come under occupation in his forthcoming Russian campaign. The SS were to have control of the dark realm of genocide and mass deportation.

1 DECEMBER   **1942**

It is always said the SS are brutal. But what else would you do? If partisans shove women and children to the front, you must be able to fire regardless.

While these acts of atrocious cruelty were carried out by the *Totenkopfverbande* (Death's Head) SS and 'special duty' squads recruited from all the other branches of the organization, the *Waffen SS* made a gradual increase in strength and importance. There were six divisions of them in the invasion of Russia—not a large number considering the titanic forces involved, but they had a disproportionate effect. Hitler had a sort of coarse affection for the men of the corps which was rather like his feeling for his dogs. He liked to belive that they were godless and loyal only to him.

He was amused by the peccadilloes of his personal guards who were found from the ranks of the *Liebstandarte* division of the *Waffen SS* .He still thought of them as tough, healthy pagans who could show the regular Army a thing or two. He did not, by then, rely on them completely.

During his lethal career Heydrich had aroused a good deal of antagonism, but his most deadly enemies turned out to be the British special services. The British had taken a no-holds-barred attitude to the use of assassination in war, and on 20 May 1942 two of their Czechoslovakian agents managed to blow up Heydrich. That Heydrich deserved the lingering death which this brought him is not in dispute but it is at least possible that it did more harm than good. A holocaust of Czechs followed the courageous deed and the ability of the multifarious agencies of the RSHA to carry on its evil work was in no whit impaired.

It also meant that Himmler and many other top Nazis were relieved of the anxiety of being murdered or disgraced by the enigmatic Heydrich. For a while, Himmler took over Heydrich's position—which could hardly be considered an improvement for the subject peoples of Europe.

As the war turned against Hitler, the *Waffen SS* became more and more important to him. Although the SS divisions were few, they were armoured and lavishly equipped. This, together with their fierce fighting spirit brought results in the Russian campaign. Hitler became more and more convinced that the pessimism of the regular Army was a stumbling block to success and became ever more impressed by the constant verve of the SS. The victory of Kharkov in March 1943 was the last great German success of the war. It came hard on the heels of Stalingrad and it was gained chiefly by the SS. From that moment on, Hitler endorsed an enormous expansion of his *Waffen SS* units. The three earliest SS divisions became Germany's crack armoured corps, and other armoured corps and divisions were soon raised. The ranks were filled by a higher proportion of Nordic Europeans and ethnic Germans than Reich Germans.

Above: *The degree of independence allowed the judiciary can be judged from this picture taken at the trial of the Stauffenberg conspirators.*

26 JULY   1943

Today I got an opinion how the *Goering* division stands up in combat. The English write that the very youngest, the 16 year olds, just out of the Hitler Youth, have fought fanatically to the last man. The English could not take any prisoners.

Part of Hitler's belief in the superiority of his SS soldiers rested on his confidence that they were fanatical Nazis. They had been exposed to intensive indoctrination during training and, in moments when he was thinking even less clearly than usual, the Fuhrer regarded them as missionaries. Their belief could bolster up Italy's faltering Fascists. Everything in Hitler's make-up warmed to the

SS ideal: they were an elite, they were loyal, they were under his personal command and they were Nazis.

Many of them had been enrolled in the Hitler Youth before joining the SS and had therefore been indoctrinated in Nazi ideals all their lives. Their fine reputation in combat was balanced by their ruthless willingness to massacre, but Hitler did not mind that. *Reichsfuhrer SS* Himmler expressed the Nazi view perfectly when he recognized that fear of the SS was useful: 'We will never let that excellent weapon, the dread and terrible reputation which preceded us in the battle for Kharkov, fade, but will constantly add new meaning to it'.

Fast though the SS grew in Hitler's favour it took another crisis to make them of paramount importance in the Third Reich. On 20 July 1944, Graf von Stauffenberg attempted to kill Hitler with a bomb and very nearly succeeded. Stauffenberg was a staff officer and had a considerable amount of rather tenuous support for his coup d'etat among senior officers of the Army. Hitler was not above personal brutality and he took pleasure in particularly merciless revenge against the plotters.

Investigations into the matter discovered that very large numbers of important officers had had some inkling of the proposed assassination. Even those who had merely heard rumours but had not passed them on were executed in a slow and painful manner.

31 AUGUST   **1944**

The fact that the conspiracy did not succeed gives us the chance to rid Germany of this cancer. If I had had the 9th and 10th SS Panzer Divisions in the West, the whole thing probably would not have happened.

Below: *In jovial mood, Himmler with Rommel in 1939. As head of the SS, Himmler was ultimately responsible for exposing Rommel as sympathetic to the Stauffenberg conspirators and ensuring that he committed suicide.*

It transpired that many of the plotters had been hoping to use the troops under their command to further the putsch. There was even an ill-defined plan for commanders in France to negotiate terms with the Western Allies. Throughout the crisis, the SS proved themselves the rock upon which Hitler's power was based. None of their officers had flirted with the plotters and, indeed, the mere presence of SS troops in any command had had an inhibiting effect on those who would be disloyal. Besides all this it was now routine to expect that where there were executions to be carried out, the SS were the men to do the dirty work.

After August 1944 fear of future plots led to a stifling SS presence around the person of the Fuhrer. At one stage when the Chief of Staff, General Guderian, attended an afternoon conference with Hitler, he and his adjutant were searched by SS men before they entered an ante-room where they waited watched by heavily armed SS guards. Sometimes, armed SS men stood behind the chair of each participant in a conference. On his last informal outing in January 1945, Hitler went to tea at Goebbel's home accompanied by six SS bodyguards who carried cakes for his personal consumption in a plastic bag. Military failure had stripped away the trappings of Hitler's power and left its naked core—the loyalty and ruthlessness of the SS.

By 1944, Himmler had created an empire which was virtually a state within a state. The story of his infamous extermination camps and concentration camps is well known, but it is not so generally realized that the SS were, to some extent, clothed and munitioned by the products

Above: *Some of Hitler's boy soldiers, seemingly happy to be captured at last. In the defence of Danzig, the SS had tried to stiffen the makeshift German forces by hanging 14-year-old boys (suspected of deserting) from the trees on the Hindenburgstrasse.*

Left: *The macabre orchestra of Auschwitz. Surrounded by indescribable human misery and degradation Himmler's camp guards liked to hear their victims play Beethoven. All the performers were later murdered.*

of SS factories run on slave labour. Nothing was beneath the RSHA. It managed brothels, an SS marriage bureau, dubious medical research projects, agencies and bank accounts for loot garnered from its murdered victims and many another sidelines. The men involved in this vast operation were more committed than most to the New Order, and military reverses only made the flame of their fanaticism blaze brighter. The hundreds of thousands of foreigners in the ranks of the *Waffen SS* would find no forgiveness after surrender and they had every inducement to fight to the end.

As the Third Reich crumbled in ruins under the effects of assaults from East and West, the Fuhrer, raving in his bunker, could still command the murderous devotion of Gestapo, SD and SS. He treated them with the same ingratitude and selfishness he showed to others.

FEBRUARY   **1945**

I believe that the troops have not fought as the situation demanded and order that the SS divisions *Adolf Hitler, Das Reich, Totenkopf* **and** *Hohenstauffen* **be stripped of their arm-bands.**

When Hitler's most famous SS divisions were cut to bits in a hopeless defence of Hungary, he castigated them and accused them of treachery and cowardice. Although some of the German SS began to lose heart at this, many of them still remained loyal and the foreigners had little alternative to fighting on. They tried to stiffen new, makeshift German forces with their brutalities—in the defence of Danzig they hanged 14-year-old boys (suspected of deserting) from the trees on the Hindenburgstrasse. On 10 September 1944, Himmler posted an order which stated: 'Certain unreliable elements seem to believe that the war will be over for them as soon as they surrender to the enemy. Every deserter will find his just punishment. Further more, his behaviour will entail the most severe consequences for his family. They will be summarily shot.'

On 6 May 1945, Himmler received his notice of dismissal from Admiral Donitz, the new Fuhrer, and a note of thanks for his services to the Reich. In the end, of course, every effort of Himmler and his 'chain-dogs' had been in vain, but surely no man was more faithfully and cruelly served than Hitler was by the institutions of terror that were the basis of his power.

Below: *Hitler reviews a parade of SS troops— the elite of the corps which he believed ultimately failed and betrayed him.*

Friends & enemies

Friends of Germany, but citizens of the country that was to prove the Reich's most powerful enemy. The American Nazi Party gained little support in the United States, and was totally disregarded by Hitler.

THE PARTY FAITHFUL

MANY OF THE FRIENDS HITLER collected in his Munich days of the *Kampfzeit* (struggle for power) were unsavoury in the extreme, but they stayed with the Fuhrer and were given positions of influence despite their shortcomings. Because he had so many of his intimates murdered, Hitler has often been accused of having a disloyal and selfish nature but this is not absolutely true. He was a dangerous and suspicious man but he did have a soft spot for his old companions and he would overlook almost any defect of character in them. His motives may not have been selfless, indeed it may simply be an indication of his own lack of moral judgement that he saw little to censure in the thugs who were his old comrades, but he was slow to abandon even the worst of them.

I know that Esser is a scoundrel but I shall hold on to him as long as he can be of use to me.

Among the first of his dubious cronies was Hermann Esser, who lived off his numerous mistresses and was a cause of scandal to many of the more fastidious members of the embryo Party. Despite everything, Hitler stuck to Esser—even when other members of the Party demanded his expulsion for depravity in 1924—and the lecherous Hermann was able to fill the undemanding post of Under-Secretary in the Propaganda Ministry after the Nazi Revolution of 1933.

28 FEBRUARY   **1941**

Despite all his weaknesses, Streicher is a man who has spirit. He put himself under my orders at a time when others were hesitating to do so. That is an unforgettable service.

8 APRIL   **1942**

Julius Streicher rendered particularly valuable service in our struggle to gain the support of the working classes. It is he whom we must thank for the capture of Nuremberg, that one-time stronghold of Marxism.

Yet, even Esser was as nothing compared to Julius Streicher—whom Hitler himself described as a lunatic. Streicher always carried a whip with him; he was a notorious sadist and womaniser, with a strong line in pornography. He was the Nazi Party's archetypal Jew-baiter, and his speeches and publications went to such disgusting, and usually obscene, lengths of anti-semitic frenzy that he turned even the strong stomachs of fellow Nazis.

Below: *Hitler justifies the struggle for Stalingrad.*
Opposite: *An appreciative audience of Nazi ministers.*

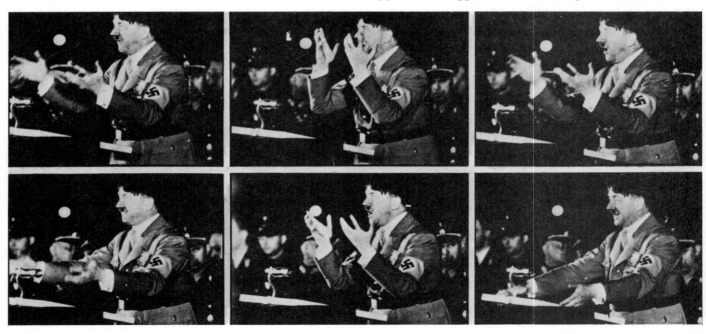

Hitler, however, never found Streicher's postures in any way excessive. Streicher's line on Jews was just commonsense to him. In any case he owed a debt to Streicher for setting his career rolling. In the very early days of the movement, Hitler's power base was restricted to Munich while other petty nationalist movements held sway in other regional centres. Streicher had a little empire in Franconia where he commanded loyal support—especially in Nuremberg. As the leader of the Nuremberg nationalists he was the first man with any personal following to join Hitler's Nazi movement. It was this first acceptance of Hitler as more than just the leader of a small sect of Munich nationalists that began the process of building the Nazi Party. For this great service Hitler was grateful and he protected Streicher from expulsion from the Party in 1924 and made him *gauleiter* of Nuremberg. However, it was to be no more than a postponement as Streicher's behaviour worsened and even Hitler could not prevent his eventual dismissal shortly before the war. In the very last days of the war, Streicher emerged from retirement—just in time to fatten the file against him at his Nuremberg trial by the Allies, (which resulted in his hanging).

Of all the human beings with whom Hitler associated, only one seemed to command his total respect and admiration. This was the journalist Dietrich Eckart who made the young Hitler his protege and moulded his early career.

1924

Eckart was one of the best who devoted his life to the awakening of our people, in his writings and his thoughts and finally in his deeds.

Eckart was a flamboyant, boozy journalist who died of drink at the end of 1923. While he lived he was the leader, wit and guide of Munich working-class nationalism. He was convinced that the nationalist movement needed a working-class leader as the German people had lost confidence in the officer class and he saw Hitler in the role of the new leader. He helped to buy the *Volkischer Beobachter*—the Party's first newspaper—and he edited it. Perhaps his death was timely in that he did not live to disappoint the future Fuhrer but remained always the object of affectionate memory and reverence.

16 JANUARY   1942

Eckart shone in our eyes like the polar star. What others wrote was so flat.

Another character who became an early member of the Nazi Party was the 'philosopher' Alfred Rosenberg. He was a rather muddled man with intellectual pretensions who also edited the *Volkischer Beobachter* for a while and turned out an unbelievably turgid and incomprehensible book enigmatically entitled *The Myth of the Twentieth Century*'.

21 AUGUST   1942

At the beginning, the *Volkischer Beobachter* sailed on so high a plane that I myself had difficulty understanding it, and I certainly know no woman who could.

Hitler was moderately fond of this bumbler in a mocking sort of way but he regarded him as something of a liability—a man completely incapable of communication with ordinary mortals. He has been described as the philosopher of the Nazi Party whose work determined the Nazi outlook, but that is placing far too much value on his contribution to the New Order.

11 APRIL   **1942**

It gives me considerable pleasure to realize that Rosenberg's book has been closely studied only by our opponents. Like most of our *gauleiters*, I have myself merely glanced cursorily at it.

Hitler always thought Rosenberg's book was something of a joke and he was probably right when he claimed that few of the top Nazis had bothered to read it. However, Rosenberg was given his piece of the action at the height of Hitler's success and he was made Commissioner for the Eastern Territories. His powers in this post were soon usurped by Himmler and others who were more ruthless and single-minded than he could ever be. Mild as he was compared to his successors, he still did enough, in his incompetent way, to earn himself a death sentence at Nuremberg.

In his early days, Hitler's strong right arm was the stormtrooper army of the SA. The men he chose to command these hooligans were not much of an advertisement for honesty and clean-living. Among his first commanders was Captain Franz Felix Pfeffer von Salomon—a man whose name sounded grand enough but who was, in Hitler's own words, 'a tramp'. Pfeffer had kicked off his post-1918 military career by raising a free-corps for the purpose of extortion.

MARCH   **1945**

Pfeffer raised a free-corps and then used it for extortion against his own government. I would have knocked ideas like that out of Pfeffer's head. I would have strung him up afterwards, but the free-corps was there.

It was simply Pfeffer's ability to raise a contingent of fighting men that interested Hitler, and once the old crook had done that he was disposable. However, finding a good commander of the SA was not easy and a number of unreliables were tried and found wanting before Hitler stumbled upon one of the most remarkable and able of his sidekicks.

3 JANUARY   **1942**

One day I had an opportunity to hear a speech by Goering, in which he declared himself resolutely on the side of German honour. I liked him. I made him the head of my SA. He is the only one of its heads who ran the SA properly. I gave him a dishevelled rabble, and, in a very short time he had organized a division of 11,000 men.

Hermann Goering was a war hero whose cluster of decorations included the *Pour le Merite*—equivalent to a British Victoria Cross or American Congressional Medal of Honour. Goering licked the SA into shape in short order and he became the most forceful and valuable of all the Nazi chieftains until his debilitation from drugs and self-indulgence. Along the way he was involved in his share of war crimes, however, but cheated the Nuremberg gallows by taking poison the night before he was due to hang.

Nazi success during the Munich days of the *Kampfzeit* owed a lot to having supporters inside the government. Chief of these was police-boss Wilhelm Frick who did his best to tilt the security forces into covert support for Hitler.

29 MARCH   **1942**

Frick conducted himself admirably as adjutant to the Chief of Police. He was able to supply us with all kinds of information which enabled the Party rapidly to expand its activity. He never missed an opportunity to help us and protect us. I can even add that, without him, I would never have got out of prison. But there exists unfortunately a particular type of National Socialist who, at a certain moment did great things for the Party, but who is never capable of doing still better.

Frick was of immense value during the days when the Party was a strictly Bavarian phenomenon and he even helped to get Hitler paroled from Landsberg prison after

Opposite: *Rank and file SS Party faithful, swear allegiance to the Fuhrer in a macabre midnight ceremony at Munich's Feldherrnhalle.*

the abortive Beer-hall Putsch. Although he coped well in such a comparatively humble position he was unable to make much of the potential powers of the Ministry of the Interior when he took it over after the Nazi Revolution. He was eventually displaced by Himmler and kicked upstairs as Protector of Bohemia and Moravia. He is often described as a colourless personality, but there was sufficient colour in his background for the Nuremberg judges to send him to the gallows.

Another future top Nazi to step from the corrupted ranks of Bavaria's officials was Judge Franz Gurtner. He presided over Hitler's trial after the Beer-hall Putsch and rendered imperishable service to injustice by his lenient conduct of that farce.

29 MARCH   **1942**

Gurtner has himself had a lot of difficulty in getting rid of his legal superstitions. If anyone thinks that I chose Gurtner as Minister of Justice because, once upon a time, in his capacity of judge, he must have treated me with particular understanding, that would not correspond with the facts. When I had to choose amongst the men in the running, I could not find anyone better.

Gurtner found his way into Hitler's 1933 cabinet as Minister of Justice but this was, as Hitler later confessed, *faute de mieux*. The Fuhrer was not fond of lawyers and Gurtner never rose very high in his esteem.

All scum floats to the surface, and many of Hitler's early comrades rose right to the top of the heap when he came to power; but there were also some who were never really given high office although they retained Hitler's friendship. Of these men, the two who came closest to being real friends of Hitler—in so far as he relaxed his guard to be on intimate terms with anyone—were Heinrich Hoffmann, who became his official photographer, and Max Amann.

24 FEBRUARY   **1942**

I know three people who, when they are together, never stop laughing. They are Amann, Hoffmann and Goebbels. I am very fond of Hoffmann . . . a man who always makes fun of me.

Neither of these two did badly out of the Party's success and Amann, who had been a sergeant-major in

Hitler's regiment during World War I, became a millionaire publisher and Head of the Party Press Department—but they were rare birds in that they were people who were close to Hitler but not really involved in the struggle for power between his greater henchmen.

After he had come to power, Hitler often looked back upon the beginnings of the *Kampfzeit* in Munich as the good old days. From those times came the men whom he called the '*alte kampfer*', the old fighters who had shared hard times with him. Chief amongst them was Rudolf Hess. Hess had been an officer in Hitler's regiment during World War I, but did not fall under the ex-corporal's spell until the early 1920s. He eventually became the closest and most devoted of Hitler's friends.

17 JANUARY   **1942**

For years I lived on Tyrolean apples and so did Hess. It is crazy what economies we had to make. Every mark saved was for the Party.

Hess and Hitler shared the privations and the triumphs of founding the Nazi movement and they were imprisoned together after the Beer-hall Putsch. In prison Hess acted as secretary to Hitler and helped him to produce his book *Mein Kampf*. He was Hitler's closest confidant and his dog-like devotion was amply rewarded. He was made Party Secretary to relieve Hitler of the burden of administration and he was named Deputy Fuhrer—Hitler's successor. With the onset of war, however, he felt that he was losing his unique position with Hitler to the soldiers and Party members more actively engaged in its prosecution. In a bid to regain the spotlight and his leader's friendship he flew to enemy Britain (leaving a rather disjointed explanatory letter behind him) and tried to negotiate a peace.

10 MAY   **1941**

I cannot recognize Hess in this letter. It is a different person. Something must have happened to him—some mental disturbance.

The British treated Hess as a lunatic, as did Hitler. He was tried at Nuremberg after the war and sentenced to life imprisonment. He is still in prison today.

When Hitler was released from prison he found his political position much altered. In his absence the Party had enjoyed considerable electoral success and had found, in the radical Gregor Strasser, a man who was virtually a rival for the Party leadership. At the same time

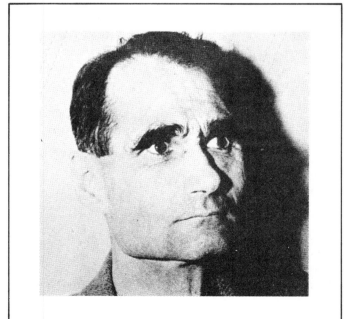

Above: *Hitler and Hess inspect the construction of the Fuhrer's new house in Munich.*
Left: *Hess, after four years in a British prison (following his ill-fated, self-imposed mission to negotiate a peace). Both Hitler and the British thought he was mad.*

a move had been afoot to expel Streicher and Esser from the Party on the grounds of their general undesirability. Hitler soon moved to protect his unwanted friends and made it plain that Nazis had to put up with each other whatever their personal feelings.

26 FEBRUARY   1925

I do not consider it to be the task of a political leader to attempt to improve upon or even to fuse together the human material lying ready to his hand.

During Hitler's imprisonment, the Party's influence had spread beyond Bavaria and had netted a new pack of knaves to join the Nazi rogues gallery—in particular a number of future *gauleiters*.

27 DECEMBER   **1943**

In every election I had districts in which I knew that, when the election came, there would be a victory there. In one place I had Koch, in the other Sauckel, and then I had Ley. I had the men.

Years later, Hitler reminisced fondly about the contribution these loathsome creatures made to his *Kampfzeit* and waxed particularly maudlin about the three nastiest—Erich Koch, *gauleiter* of East Prussia, Fritz Sauckel, *gauleiter* of Thuringia and Robert Ley, *gauleiter* of the Rhineland.

Erich Koch was always looked upon as a pretty hard case by Hitler himself. He was a man who could sort the Nazi sheep from the goats. As a result of his hard-driving policies, he was made Reich Commissar for the Ukraine during the period of triumph in the East. He summed up his role fairly accurately in a speech at Kiev on 5 March 1943. 'I will draw the very last out of this country for I did not come to spread bliss. We are a master race which must remember that the lowliest German worker is racially and biologically a thousand times more valuable than the population here'. After the war he was handed over to the Polish government for a richly deserved hanging but was temporarily reprieved on account of illness. Amazingly, he was still clinging to life in a prison hospital in 1979.

The bulging, piggy-eyed Fritz Sauckel was also a red-hot organizer. Hitler recognized this ability and gave him the opportunity to organize one of the greatest crimes in history—the Reich's slave labour programme. In this capacity he was more than a shade wasteful as so many of his unwilling workers died from starvation, maltreatment, cold or untreated diseases. He summed up his attitude to them in his famous phrase 'There is no claim to free time'.

21 AUGUST   **1942**

Sauckel told me a very curious fact. All the girls whom we bring back from the Eastern territories are medically examined and 25 per cent of them are found to be virgins. That could not happen in Upper Bavaria.

Sauckel shared with Hitler the rather degrading view that his human slaves were simply so many statistics—things of no value which could be subjected to any indignity. He was one of the ten top Nazis to be dropped into the next world through the trapdoor of the Nuremberg prison gallows.

Robert Ley was qualified as a chemist but handicapped by a stammer and a drink problem. He was made Head of the Party Organization after the fall of Gregor Strasser in 1933. After his arrest of Trade Union leaders, Ley's German Labour Front compulsorily enrolled every German worker. His efforts to represent the workers against their employers were negligible and his phrase 'Only the employer can decide' shows which side his sympathies were on.

28 FEBRUARY   **1942**

I have a man, Robert Ley, to whom it will be enough for me to entrust this mission . .

Above: *Hitler visits the Volkswagen factory to inspect a production model of the new 'people's car'. Thousands paid 5 marks a week for the car, but none was delivered. Robert Ley was the entrepreneur behind the scheme.*

Hitler showed a touching faith in Ley's ability to manage great projects, but his only real talent was for fraud. He was the man who got the Volkswagen project rolling by the happy idea of making the workers pay in advance for the cars they were to receive—of course, no cars were ever delivered and no money was ever refunded. There were a lot of other ways in which his accounts did not bear inspection and he opted out of appearing before the Nuremberg judges by hanging himself in his cell.

Another recruit of 1925 was Paul Joseph Goebbels—eventual *gauleiter* of Berlin and Reich's Minister for Propaganda, one of the half-dozen very top Nazis. He was originally introduced to the Party by the radical Gregor Strasser. Although Hitler won Goebbels over from the Strasser faction in 1925, radicalism in the Party continued to be a problem until the Night of the Long Knives in 1934.

21 MAY   1942

After the vain and treacherous attempts of General Schleicher, supported by Gregor Strasser, had failed to split the Party, political tension reached its zenith.

The radicals were those who attached a degree of importance to the word Socialist in the official Nazi Party title of National Socialist Party. Strasser never really made use of his influence within the Party to challenge Hitler for the leadership and when he finally broke with Hitler in December 1932 he made no attempt to split the Party but resigned and went on holiday to Italy. Hitler settled accounts when he had him murdered the next year.

The truly titanic battle over radicalism came between Goering and Hitler's oldest supporter Ernst Rohm. Rohm had been an officer in the Reichswehr who had been practically the first man to extend support for Hitler in his earliest Munich days. A bull-necked, scar-faced homosexual who had risen from the ranks, he was a professional tough guy whose only interest was in soldiering. He left the Army to take part in the Beer-hall Putsch and became leader of the SA while Goering, who was wounded in the Putsch, recovered in Sweden. In the mid-1920s Rohm left Germany for a military career in South America but, in January 1931, he answered an appeal from his old friend Hitler to return and restore some discipline to the SA. He took over 100,000 mutinous men, but within a year could field 300,000 disciplined troops—all too scared of him to move out of line.

By the time Hitler came to power Rohm had 3,000,000 stormtroopers whose top commanders belonged to the very rough, mainly homosexual, gang of which Rohm was the leader. They were dissatisfied with the course of the Nazi Revolution because they believed that every institution of the old state should be destroyed and Nazified—especially the Army which should be replaced by the SA. They were opposed by Goering, who was more conservative and who knew that Rohm's crew planned to murder him, and secretly by Himmler, the mild mannered but sinister police chief who resented the fact that his SS forces were under Rohm's command.

In this struggle, Hitler hardly knew which way to jump. Rohm was an old friend and doughty companion of the *Kampfzeit* and, in the first few months after his accession to power, he seemed to favour his ambitions.

7 MAY 1933

The SA has been up until now the Guard of the National Revolution. It must be the guarantor of the victorious completion of this Revolution, and it will be victoriously completed if, through the schooling of the SA, a new German people is educated.

Soon, however, Hitler was given warning that the only German institution he really respected—the Army—was not prepared to be taken over by Rohm's roughnecks. Although Rohm's 3,000,000 brownshirts should, in theory, have been able to deal with the 100,000 men of the Reichswehr, Hitler was taking no risks when he was within fingertip reach of absolute power. By 1 July 1933 he was issuing reassurances to the Army.

1 JULY 1933

This army of the political soldiers of the German Revolution has no wish to take the place of our Army or to enter into competition with it.

Unfortunately, Rohm and his brownshirt clique were not prepared to abandon their radical fervour or their hooligan behaviour. In the early summer of 1933 the SA had been particularly unrestrained and there were outbreaks of looting and kidnapping all over Germany as the stormtroopers levelled the rich and lined their pockets in their own untutored way. This brought up the prospect of a Germany drifting into anarchy and, on 6 July, Hitler made it clear that the general disorder must stop.

6 JULY 1933

The revolution is not a permanent state of affairs, and it must not be allowed to develop into such a state.

From August 1933 the behaviour of the SA improved but they were still straining at the leash. Rohm and his circle still believed in the nationalization of big business and incorporation of the Army into the SA and they probably believed that this was in accordance with Hitler's own views. They recognized the resourceful Goering with his upper class connections as their enemy but they underestimated him and failed to see that Himmler was giving his support to Goering. In any case, how could Goering deal with 3,000,000 stormtroopers? Their attitude seemed justified by the year's end when Rohm was apparently accepted as the Fuhrer's right-hand man—the only Nazi chieftain Hitler addressed by the familiar German *du*.

1 JANUARY 1934

At the close of the year of National Socialist Revolution, I feel compelled to thank you, my dear Ernst Rohm, for the imperishable services you have rendered to the National Socialist movement and the German people, and to assure you how very grateful I am to fate that I am able to call such men as you my friends and fellow combatants.

It is probable that the SA leaders were indeed planning another revolution but it is unlikely that they posed any threat to Hitler's life. They wanted Goering and his reactionary friends out of the way and a new socialist Germany with Hitler as Chancellor. However, Goering and Himmler set out to scare Hitler into fearing for his life. Goering retained control of the Prussian state police (*Landespolizeigruppe*) and they managed to bug the telephones of the SA leadership which allowed Goering to show highly selective bits of their conversations to Hitler. Himmler's Gestapo built up photographs and files of the SA homosexuals indulging their sexual appetites and listed the numerous complaints of parents whose children had been raped or abducted by them. Hitler was not normally upset by this sort of lusty behaviour but it provided a further irritant. A final push came from President Hindenburg and Defence Minister Blomberg who made it clear that the Army would not tolerate amalgamation with the SA.

4 JUNE   **1934**

I implored Rohm for the last time to oppose this madness of his own accord, to use his authority to stop a development which could only end in catastrophe.

Uncertain how to act, Hitler tried to defuse the situation by reasoning with Rohm and it was agreed that the whole SA would go on leave for the month of July. Rohm himself went on sick leave on 7 June but not until he had issued a warning: 'If the foes of the SA are nursing the hope that the SA will not return from their leave, they will receive the fitting answer. The SA is and remains Germany's destiny.'

While Rohm and some of his most unpleasant friends relaxed with various handsome male companions at a health resort on Lake Wiesse, Goering and Himmler kept the pressure on Hitler until he made up his mind on 29 June 1934.

Once pushed over the brink, Hitler worked himself up into a splendid state of hysteria and was practically frothing at the mouth when his plane landed at Munich, early on 30 June, and he emerged to lambast the various SA leaders who were brought to him under SS guard. Invigorated by this, he set off for Lake Wiesse surrounded by a brutish crew of SS toughs and burst in on Rohm and his entourage. One SA boss and his youthful male lover were dragged out and shot on the spot, Hitler lashed about in a satisfying way with his whip and Rohm and various others were carted off and murdered in Munich.

In Berlin, the busy Goering, supported by the Army and his police, had snatched the rest of the SA leadership and put them in front of an SS firing squad. There was no slackening the next day and the executions continued while Hitler held a decorous tea party in the Chancellery gardens. The official death toll was 73 but in fact it ran into hundreds and the threat from the SA was snuffed out for ever. Hitler was congratulated by Hindenburg for murdering his friends and the whole colourful episode was dubbed 'The Night of the Long Knives'—because, it has been said, the SS who carried out the murders were distinctively equipped with sizeable daggers.

Shortly after Rohm's liquidation, Hindenburg died and

Above: *Hitler preaching duty and loyalty to a gathering of the Party faithful in pre-war Berlin.*

Hitler added the Presidency to his Chancellorship. The abrupt demise of the SA leadership proved no deterrent to the new candidates for power ready to swarm out of the woodwork and relieve Hitler of the burden of administration. One such individual was the bright young lawyer Hans Frank, who had joined the Party in 1927. In spite of Hitler's proven contempt for legality, Frank still made a career for himself in the Nazi hierarchy. In the 30s he became Commissioner for Justice and Reich Law Leader and encouraged his fellow lawyers to abandon all restraints and simply obey the will of the Fuhrer. After the conquest of Poland, he was made Governor General of that unhappy land.

5 APRIL   **1942**

It was agreed with Frank that the Kracow district and also the Lublin district should be peopled by Germans. Once these two spots have been strengthened it should be possible to drive the Polish population slowly back.

Spurred on by Hitler's interest, Frank embarked on a programme of extreme cruelty towards Poland's population. He showed an almost insane bloodthirstiness: 'If I wished to order that a poster be hung up for every seven Poles shot,' he raved, 'there would not be enough forests in Poland to make the paper for those posters'. For all his legal skills, however, Frank was found guilty of war crimes at Nuremberg and hanged.

Hitler had no real interest in economics but after he came to power he was particularly well served by the brilliant financier Hjalmar Schacht who was made Minister for Economics. Their relationship was not a happy one. Although Schacht was quite as enthusiastic as anyone else for rearming Germany, he was practically the only man who dared to argue with Hitler.

16 AUGUST   **1942**

I have never had a conference with Schacht to find out what means were at our disposal. I restricted myself to saying simply 'this is what I require and this is what I must have.' Schacht always opposed me on principle, but I was more than a match for Herr Schacht. These financiers seem to have no idea of the real efficiency of economic principles.

Hitler was not prepared to listen to the voice of reason and Schacht resigned in December 1937. During the war he became involved in one of the plots against Hitler and he ended up in a concentration camp. He was lucky to survive to be acquitted at Nuremberg.

27 JANUARY   **1942**

Whatever I did, things did not go forward. Things only began to change at the Ministry of Economics when Funk took it in hand.

Schacht was succeeded by the nonentity Walther Funk who the Fuhrer could walk over at will. Although Funk kept on the right side of Hitler, he ended up with a sentence of life imprisonment from the judges at Nuremberg for his part in managing the SS account which made deposits of the gold teeth taken from dead Jews.

While Hitler was uninterested in finance he was passionately concerned with breeding new soldiers and he entrusted the Hitler Youth to Baldur von Schirach. From 1933 this clean-cut, semi-American was made 'Youth Leader of the German Reich' and he set the nations boys and girls to play at soldiers in readiness for the day when play would become reality.

Below: *Albert Speer explaining his architect's model of an area of the new Germany. Speer was eventually promoted to masterminding the Reich's munition supply—something which undoubtedly extended the life of the war. It was for this he received a 20-year sentence at Nuremberg.*

I cannot help congratulating myself for having found in Schirach the ideal man for the leadership of the National Socialist Youth Movement. To Schirach undoubtedly belongs the credit for having founded and organized on the most solid basis the most important youth movement in the world.

Hitler looked upon Schirach as a model for the younger generation and did not hesitate to promote him to higher office. After the *Anschluss* he was made Governor and *gauleiter* of Vienna. By Nazi standards he was not particularly cruel but it was while he was in control of Vienna that the Jewish population was deported and, largely, murdered. For the part he played in the Reich, the Allies sentenced Schirach to 20 years imprisonment after the war.

Once Hitler had come to power, he could indulge his rather individual taste for the arts. He had always been interested in architecture—indeed, when he drew or sketched, his subjects were always buildings—and the young architect Albert Speer became his favourite protege. Speer graduated from designing the Fuhrer's offices to helping stage-manage the annual titanic display at the Nuremberg rallies. He was a man who remained somewhat outside the back-biting circles of the Nazi hierarchy and he could not fail to be dismayed by the staggering inefficiency with which that crew of incompetents ran the war effort.

Transportation of goods hither and thither all over Germany, as Speer recently proved to me with voluminous graphs, is sheer idiocy. This chaos must come to an end. It is nonsense that cigarettes manufactured in Dresden should be sent to Berlin for distribution and then that a proportion of them, representing the ration for Saxony, should solemnly be sent back to Dresden again.

In a rare moment of sense at the beginning of 1942 Hitler made him Minister of Armament and War Production, where he achieved wonders in straightening out the mess bequeathed him. It is not too much to say

that Speer's efforts averted a disaster to the German war effort and enabled the struggle to be continued. Much of this miracle was achieved through the extensive use of slave labour and, for that, Speer was also sentenced to 20 years after the war.

It went without saying that, once Germany became a totalitarian state, Hitler would come to rely upon the services of his special police forces. The man who owned this empire was, of course, Heinrich Himmler, who had taken part in the Beer-hall Putsch but was slow to emerge as a man of importance. Hitler acknowledged that Himmler had a way with policemen, but he was not in the first rank of Nazi satraps until after the Rohm purge. Even then it seemed to many that the cold, blond Reinhard Heydrich who was in charge of the SD was a far more formidable and ruthless proposition than Himmler. However, Heydrich had a weakness for driving around in an open car without an escort in occupied territory and he died at the hands of assassins on 4 June 1942.

That a man as irreplaceable as Heydrich should expose himself to unnecessary danger I can only condemn as stupid and idiotic.

Hitler was irritated that a man as 'irreplaceable' as Heydrich should have been lax enough to get himself killed. In the end it was found that Heydrich was not irreplaceable at all and, after Himmler had held down his job for a while, it was passed on to Ernst Kaltenbrunner. Kaltenbrunner was thoroughly immersed in all the atrocities undertaken by his department and it was no surprise at all when the Allies sentenced him to be hanged after the war.

While his henchmen busied themselves in the rewarding work of running Germany and her conquests, Hitler had a need for diplomats to manage affairs abroad. He inherited Constantin von Neurath, a diplomat of the old school, from the Weimar Republic and set him to work projecting a reassuringly conservative image. The trouble was that Neurath was not really enough of a Nazi to suit the Fuhrer and in February 1938 he was replaced at the Foreign Office by the eminently dislikeable Joachim von Ribbentrop. After Czechoslovakia had been dismembered later that year, Neurath was made Protector of Bohemia and Moravia.

Neurath never seems to have been a committed Nazi—at least in Hitler's eyes—but enough hardship was imposed on the Czechs to drag him before the Allied judges at Nuremberg and get him 15 years imprisonment.

Everyone, including Hitler, was agreed that Ribbentrop was a particularly nasty piece of work—but Hitler was convinced, quite wrongly, that Ribbentrop was a states-

man of genius. Ribbentrop's main hatred in life seems to have been the British, who gave him a feeling of inferiority. Goering was always certain that it was this hatred, allied to incompetence, which succeeded in bringing Germany and Britain to war. Goering was a passionate enemy of Ribbentrop, who must have been a very lonely man—from the records it does seem that absolutely no one liked him. Despite Hitler's opinion he really was not much of a hand at diplomacy.

At the time of the first Japanese victories it did seem to Hitler that Ribbentrop had found him an ally that could counterbalance the United States, but both of them were totally ignorant of the reality of American strength and the sort of thing that was likely to happen when the US started to hit out. For his very large share in planning and starting the war, Ribbentrop was the first of the condemned Nazis to hang at Nuremberg—on 16 October 1946.

Once Hitler began on his career of territorial aggrandisement all sorts of quislings and Nazi sympathisers clambered onto the gravy train. The archetype of these was perhaps Artur Seyss-Inquart, the Austrian Nazi who helped foment the internal conditions necessary for the *Anschluss*. His reward was to be made Reich Com-

Left: *Ribbentrop, the first Nazi to hang at Nuremberg.*
Below: *Those of the Nazi hierarchy sentenced to hang at Nuremberg.*

Artur Seyss-Inquart   *Fritz Sauckel*   *Ernst Kaltenbrunner*   *Julius Streicher*   *Hans Frank*

Alfred Jodl   *Alfred Rosenberg*   *Wilhelm Frick*   *Martin Bormann*   *Wilhelm Keitel*

missioner in the Netherlands when they came under the German heel.

27 FEBRUARY   **1942**

I need an extraordinarily clever man, as supple as an eel, amiable—and at the same time thick-skinned and tough. I have in Seyss-Inquart a man who has these qualities.

Hitler thought that Seyss-Inquart was an amiable man as well as a tough one. It was, however, his tough side that made the most impression on the judges at Nuremberg, and they sentenced him to death.

Hitler's obsession with all things military meant that his interest in the armed forces was personal. It was not enough for him to give the orders to rearm or to overrun whichever country was next on his list, he liked to immerse himself in the planning and control of all campaigns. His position as Supreme Commander of the Armed Forces was, in theory, an honorary one—like that of the King of England or the President of the United States—but he concerned himself closely with the progress of rearmament. In early 1938, the Commander in Chief of the Armed Forces and the Commander in Chief of the Army were involved in sexual scandals—which were probably arranged by Goering and Himmler—and, on 4 February, Hitler replaced them and their function with a High Command of the Armed Forces which he ran himself. However, he needed staff officers to assist him in his new position and he found it consistently difficult to get along with many of his generals for long. There were two exceptions: General (later Fieldmarshal) Wilhelm Keitel, who became Chief of Staff of the new organization with the grand title of Chief of the High Command, and General Alfred Jodl, who became its Chief of Operations.

22 JULY   **1942**

Jodl is quite right when he says that notices in the Ukrainian language 'Beware of the Trains' are superfluous; what on earth does it matter if one or two more locals get run over by trains?

In Keitel and Jodl, Hitler had found two military toadies who only rarely disagreed with him and who were almost his constant companions throughout the war. After the war, because of their positions, they were judged to have acquiesced in a number of war crimes and were hanged. It seems, however, that Jodl was the more

actively callous of the two and that Keitel was little more than a weary shadow who meekly agreed with everything the Fuhrer said.

While the Fuhrer's relationship with the Army was not the feast of reason and flow of soul that each side might have desired, the Navy gave far less cause for dissatisfaction. In a sense this was inevitable because Hitler had not the slightest real interest in the Navy's function and therefore did not make upon it the impossible demands which he made on the Army. Mutual understanding was enhanced by the Navy's enthusiasm for Nazism. Admiral Raeder who commanded the Navy during Germany's rearmament was absolutely delighted by the Nazi emphasis on the Armed Forces and gave Hitler every support.

17 DECEMBER   **1941**

What a fine thing it is the war-flag of the Reich. But it is only used by the Navy. Raeder knows that when a ship hoists its colours, it is hoisting the colours of the nation.

Hitler, for his part, felt that Raeder was one of the few military men who understood Nazism and its fierce nationalist commitment. However, even the Navy could not escape censure when the Fuhrer was in one of his less rational moods. On 1 January Hitler ordered the breakup of the surface ships of the Navy on the grounds that they had been unable to take on the Royal Navy and, in particular, halt the British Arctic convoys. In response to this, Raeder resigned on 6 January and was succeeded by Admiral Karl Doenitz, another good Nazi, who was a specialist in submarine warfare. Doenitz was the only one of Hitler's commanders to retain his confidence to the end and, as a reward for this talented exercise, he was made the Fuhrer's direct successor in the last testament which the dictator made a few hours before his death.

29 APRIL   **1945**

I appoint Admiral Doenitz as president of the Reich and Supreme Commander of the Armed Forces.

As convinced Nazis who had connived in the construction of the Third Reich's war machine, both Raeder and Doenitz appeared before the Nuremberg judges at the end of the war. The British, who had suffered the greatest losses in lives and cargo from their efforts, were particularly hostile. Raeder was given a life sentence and Doenitz 10 years imprisonment.

TRAITORS & ASSASSINS

NOT ALL THE OPPOSITION TO HITLER came from abroad. There were a number of Germans ranging from clergymen to students whose consciences prevented them from accepting his regime. But perhaps the longest-standing and most significant opposition centred around the many non-Nazi senior soldiers who had been retired in 1938, when Hitler tightened his hold on the Army. The most determined of them was probably General Ludwig Beck and he was soon immersed in a web of resistance organized by Carl Goerdeler, the mayor of Leipzig. The conspirators, who included many noblemen, enjoyed extraordinary connections with officers who were still serving Hitler. They were able to approach many of Hitler's Fieldmarshals who, while still unwilling to take decisive action against the Fuhrer, did not betray their confidences.

3 MAY   **1942**

In the two really dangerous attempts made to assassinate me, I owe my life not to the police but to pure chance. On 9 November 1939 I left the Burgerbrau ten minutes before the appointed time, because of an urgent conference in Berlin.

In the early years of the war there were a number of uncoordinated and unlikely attempts on Hitler's life—the bomb blast in the *Burgerbrau* on 9 November 1939 may even have been organized by the Gestapo for their own mysterious reasons. As time wore on, the determination of the plotters to kill Hitler hardened and they began to receive less discouragement from serving soldiers.

After more than one failed attempt, the conspirators had a stroke of luck when Lt. Col. Count Klaus von Stauffenberg, one of their number, was given a staff job with occasional access to Hitler's conferences at his headquarters in East Prussia. On 20 July 1944, Stauffenberg beiefly attended one such conference—staying just long enough to push his briefcase and the bomb it contained under the conference table. Outside, he waited for the explosion, telephoned the good news to Berlin and made off. Unfortunately, not long after Stauffenberg's departure, a singed, but otherwise unhurt, Fuhrer emerged from the rubble. It took some time for the Nazi top brass to work out what had happened and who was responsible but news soon came in of an attempted putsch in Berlin.

Opposite: *Lt. Col. Count Klaus von Stauffenberg, the man who came nearest to killing Hitler.*

20 JULY   **1944**

I will put their wives and children into concentration camps and show them no mercy.

Hitler was instilled with a rancorous desire for revenge, and his survival—added to the rather halting plans of the conspirators—ensured that the revolt was shortlived. The SS and Gestapo were soon in full swing. When it became clear that the coup had failed, Stauffenberg was shot and Beck allowed to commit suicide by General Friedrich Fromm, who had flirted with the conspiracy and was later executed himself by the SS.

A number of other conspirators, including the retired Fieldmarshal von Witzleben, were hanged slowly with piano wire (a sequence that was filmed so that Hitler could watch it) but it was not so simple to deal with those of the high ranking officers in France who had been involved. It could not be pretended that the coup had been an isolated affair concerning only a few disaffected officers when it was apparent that many very senior officers on the western front were involved—General Karl von Stuelpnagel had even arrested all the SS and SD in Paris before he heard that the plot had failed. Stuelpnagel was executed but the Gestapo scented that the plot went even higher—to the serving Fieldmarshals themselves.

31 AUGUST   **1944**

Fieldmarshal Kluge committed suicide. There are strong reasons to suspect that, had he not committed suicide, he would have been arrested anyway. The manner of his involvement may have been tragic. Perhaps he just slipped into it; I do not know. If one looks at these people, Stieff and the others, their level is really incredibly low.

When Fieldmarshal von Kluge, Commander in Chief West, was ordered to return home he knew what to expect and committed suicide. Hitler's malevolence was incredible, nearly 7,000 conspirators are believed to have perished in various atrocious ways. However, a certain subtlety was called for to deal with the biggest fish of all—Fieldmarshal Erwin Rommel.

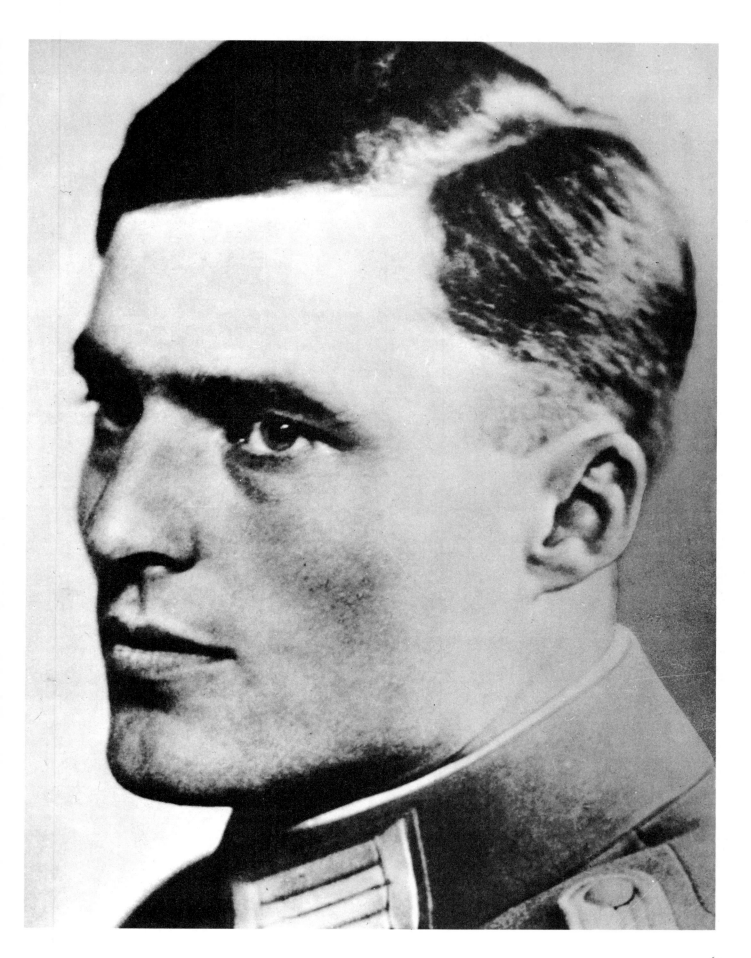

The name of Fieldmarshal Rommel will be for ever linked with the heroic battles in North Africa.

Rommel was a national hero and he had agreed to lend his name to a new government after Hitler's fall. He was recovering from wounds at the time of the plot and the SS found him at home. So great was his prestige that Hitler did not want his disaffection to be known—but he still wanted him dead. In exchange for the safety of his family, Rommel agreed to commit suicide and it was given out that he had died of wounds. To cover the traces further, Rommel was given a hero's funeral complete with a mendacious tribute from the Fuhrer himself.

The barbarities which followed the plot of 20 July 1944 effectively put an end to internal resistance to Hitler, and the bloodshed which was known as the 'Night of the Generals' humbled the Army. However, the point remained that many of the senior soldiers had only become involved in the conspiracy because they knew that military disaster was not far off. When that military disaster finally came and the ties of fear or gratitude which had bound so many to their Fuhrer were loosened even the Nazi inner circle deserted Hitler's doomed cause. In the last nightmare days of the Reich both Goering and Himmler tried to negotiate with the Allies and, for that, became Hitler's enemies.

Even from the bunker, Hitler tried to reach out and destroy these old comrades. Goaded by the sinister Party Secretary Martin Bormann, who had based his power for years on being Hitler's constant companion and administrative right arm, the message went out to the SS from beleaguered Berlin 'The traitors must be exterminated. Men, do your duty!' But the Fuhrer's power to harm had waned and both Himmler and Goering reached Allied custody before they committed suicide.

Opposite: *Hitler's wrecked headquarters in East Prussia, following the failed attempt to assassinate him.*
Right: *Rommel, eventually exposed as sympathetic to the conspirators, was persuaded to commit suicide in exchange for a hero's funeral and the safety of his family.*
Below: *A sight denied the Stauffenberg conspirators— reputedly the last picture taken of Hitler, following his suicide.*

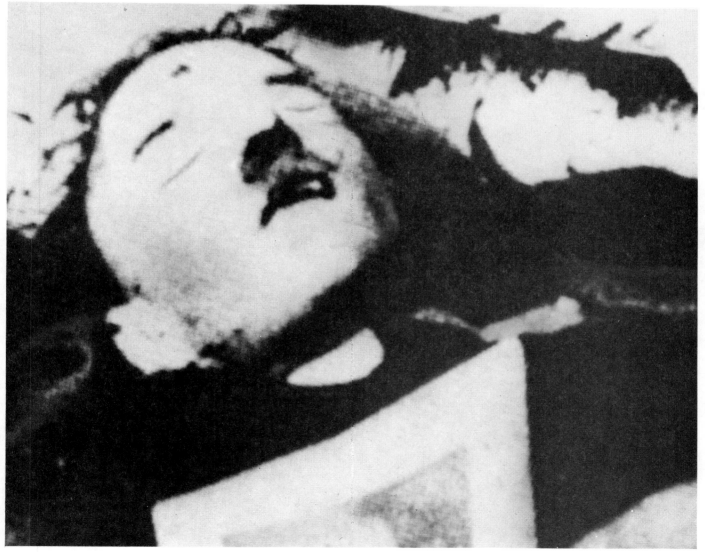

EVA BRAUN

EVEN SOME OF HITLER'S close friends were mystified by his sex-life in that they were not sure that it existed. Girl friends certainly existed and Hitler was fond of women—so long as they were not intelligent—in a sort of hand-kissing, inactive way. In conversation he often showed a certain coarse approval for rather indiscriminate sex, especially when it was likely to result in the production of more German children, but he never showed any desire to have progeny of his own. Nowadays public figures take care that their conventional tastes in sexual matters should become known, but Hitler cultivated an air of mystery as though marriage and family life would reduce his ability to appear as a man of destiny. Because he felt that normal human relationships would be counted as frailty there are many who have thought him either impotent or diseased. In fact all theories are really guesses but the story of his attachments fits the idea of a megalomaniac to whom sex or love were much less important than they are to most people.

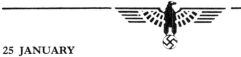

25 JANUARY   1942

What lovely women there are in the world. In my youth in Vienna I knew a lot of lovely women.

Hitler himself made occasional claim to being a ladies' man and to being quite a roguish operator in his Vienna days, but it was not until he had been released from prison after the Beer-hall Putsch that his amorous career is recorded. During that time of his life, while he was something of a celebrity but not yet burdened with power, a number of beautiful, star-crazed women such as the English Unity Mitford sought him out. All the evidence is that Hitler enjoyed only superficial relationships with these women although, after 1925, he was deeply involved in a tragic affair with his niece Geli Raubal.

Below: *Possibly an early rival of Eva Braun, the wife of a Party official pictured with Hitler in the Chancellory in 1939. Hitler enjoyed the company of women, so long as they had no intellectual pretensions.*
Opposite: *A still from a home movie Eva had taken of her. Her diary suggests she was mostly lonely and unhappy.*

At this period (1927-1930) I knew a lot of women. Several of them became attached to me. Why, then, did I not marry? To leave a wife behind me? At the slightest imprudence I ran the risk of going back to prison for six years so there could be no question of marriage for me. I therefore had to renounce certain opportunities that offered themselves.

As he later stated, Hitler enjoyed the attachments of this time but always avoided marriage. With Geli, however, things were different. She was much younger than Hitler—only 17 in 1925—but he soon had her installed in

his Munich flat and Obersalzberg house. It seems that, for Geli, the relationship may have been too intense and there were rumours that Hitler had unnatural and degrading sexual desires to which she could not respond. Hitler was intensely jealous and furious when he found that Geli had made love with his chauffeur. After a row on 17 September 1931, she shot herself while Hitler was out of Munich.

The suicide made a deep impression on Hitler, and threatened suicide was to become one of the chief weapons of his more famous mistress Eva Braun. Eva worked in the shop of Heinrich Hoffmann, Hitler's friend and official photographer. She was a pretty but brainless blonde—just Hitler's type—and, at the start, it seems that he occasionally invited her to be one of his party on an outing or sent her flowers but was not closely attached to her. However, even if Hitler was not really interested, Eva was. In the summer of 1932, when she was 21, she attempted suicide. Less than a year after Geli's death, Hitler was sensitive to that sort of gesture.

1 FEBRUARY   **1943**

When you consider that a woman has the pride to leave, to lock herself in and to shoot herself right away just because she has heard a few insulting remarks, then I cannot have any respect for a soldier who is afraid of that.

A sort of obsession over suicide seems to have been part of Hitler's make up: in the rambling, half-crazed monologue with which he reacted to his greatest disaster—Fieldmarshal Paulus's surrender at Stalingrad—he repeatedly compared Paulus's survival with the readiness of women to take their own lives, and at least one of the examples he cited closely paralleled his experience with Geli.

Eva's initiative was successful and she was soon, despite the disapproval of her parents, installed in Hitler's flat and his house. Hoffmann, who knew as much as most, reckoned that she was even then not his mistress in the physical sense. Hoffmann was equally certain that, before the end, Hitler and Eva did become lovers but could make no guess as to how long it had taken to reach that stage.

Hitler's secrecy over his affair with Eva must certainly have made her short life miserable. She had no official position and so could not be seen at Hitler's side. She was not allowed to his headquarters during the war so most of her time was spent in waiting for very brief visits from her demon lover. If she was resentful of this, it was not because she had any lust for power or position. She was a simple soul whose main interests were sport, sex and the cinema—she really does seem to have been a very nice person. At the end, when the Reich was crumbling, she

seized her chance to prove her devotion and flew into Berlin to be by Hitler's side in the last days. Her loyalty survived even the suspicious Fuhrer's brutal execution of her brother-in-law on the day before he married her. The wedding itself was simply a gesture, a reward to Eva for 'many years of true friendship' and it was carried out in the early hours of 29 April.

28 APRIL   **1945**

Although during the years of struggle I believed that I could not undertake the responsibility of marriage, now, before the end of my life, I have decided to take as my wife the woman who, after many years of true friendship, came to this city, already almost besieged, of her own free will in order to share my fate.

Eva did not have long to enjoy the married status she had sought so ardently; both she and Hitler committed suicide on 30 April and their bodies were burned to prevent them falling into the hands of the advancing Russian troops.

GOERING

OF ALL THE TOP NAZIS, GOERING was probably the man most responsible for the success of Hitler's *Kampfzeit*. The bosses of the Third Reich displayed such breathtaking seediness or fifth-rateness that Goering, a brutal and decisive man of action, made a contrast with the general run of Hitler's cronies. Although he was distinguished by his ability, he was at one with cranks like Himmler in being decidedly eccentric. For Goering's achievements and energy were eventually undermined by drug addiction, a gross and comic love of display and mental instability.

Goering's degeneration had not begun when he first met Hitler in 1922. He was a handsome, athletic war hero who had been the last commander of the famous Richthofen squadron and had earned the *Pour le Merite* and the Iron Cross First Class—Germany's two highest decorations for valour. In 1922 Goering had just returned to Germany from Sweden where he had met his beautiful and impossibly romantic first wife Karin. Although Goering belonged to the officer caste—not always a passport to favour in the embryo Nazi Party—Hitler recognized and respected him for a real fighting man. Goering the dashing hero was not content just to lend the lustre of his name to the Party but concentrated in knocking the bully boys of the SA into shape as a disciplined fighting force.

During the Beer-hall Putsch, Hitler saw Goering's ruthlessness in action. At the first police road-block Goering threatened to murder various hostages unless the Nazi column was allowed through. It worked, and Goering was not one of those who ran from the fire of the second police cordon—he was lying in the street badly wounded. These wounds—in the hip and groin—changed Goering's life: during treatment for them he became addicted to morphine. Withdrawal from drugs drove him into straitjacketed frenzy in the padded cell of a Stockholm lunatic asylum. He was never completely cured for, even after his return to Germany in 1927, he was accustomed to taking over 30 paracodeine tablets a day.

Still, Hitler knew that Goering was a man to be relied on when the chips were down and he was to prove that time and again over the coming years. During the run up to the final election that gave Hitler power, it was Goering, who had control of the Prussian police, who showed what a totally unprincipled man could do when he wielded a little of the authority of the state. It was Goering who arranged the arrest of enough opposition deputies to gain Hitler's needed majority. It was Goering, above all, who pushed Hitler into the political bloodshed of the Night of the Long Knives in 1934.

Rohm and the radicals had fully expected to have the pleasure of executing Goering. As it turned out, it was Goering who padded through cells crammed with arrested brownshirts pointing out those destined for the firing squad. His habits of wearing makeup, changing rapidly from one exotic costume to the next and of riotous over-indulgence had made his enemies underestimate him; but, when it came to the crunch, no one was more purposeful or more deadly.

Goering's trouble was that his talent for action and no-holds-barred in-fighting did not translate into ability for administration. Part of the Third Reich's weakness was that the political bandits who had served the Party well in the *Kampfzeit* were incapable of holding office in power. The two main jobs that were handed to Goering were the construction of a German air force and the control of the economic Four Year Plan. In both he produced the appearance of success but the reality was different. Goering's approach to economics was as buccaneering as everything else about him, and the German economy was set firmly in the hands of blunderers and crooks who would have brought disaster if war had not intervened. As it was, disaster was only averted when Goering retired from the fray and left Albert Speer to pick up the mess in 1942.

It was Goering's failure as creator of the Luftwaffe that brought about his downfall. Once again, he gave an initial impression of brilliant achievement which was soured by reality. The Luftwaffe of 1939 and 1940 seemed invincible enough in Poland and France where its advanced techniques of close support for ground troops were highly successful. However, in the realm of pure air combat, which was what counted in the Battle of Britain, the Luftwaffe acquitted itself honourably but found success elusive. Behind this lay a grim history of technical muddle. The British, largely unprepared for war, had an understandable shortage of pilots. The Germans, who had been preparing for years, had an unforgivable shortage of planes and were producing only 375 fighters a month. Goering had failed again.

5 JANUARY   1942

A few days before our entry into Russia I told Goering that we were facing the severest test in our existence. Goering fell off his perch, for he had been regarding the campaign in Russia as another mere formality.

At his Nuremberg trial Goering maintained that he had opposed Hitler's attack on Russia because he knew that a war on two fronts would be fatal for the Reich. Hitler's

version was different and more likely to be true—Goering could be tough enough with others but he never breathed a word of opposition to Hitler. The war on two fronts did turn out badly and particularly for the Luftwaffe. Goering's creation could not give the Russians a hammering and cope with the vengeful British at the same time—particularly when the British were joined by the Americans. By this time Goering's interest in the war appeared to have dwindled and he spent little time at the Fuhrer's endless conferences. Hitler's exasperation at his subordinate's unreliability boiled over after the night of 30 May 1942 when the RAF dropped 1500 tons of bombs on Cologne. Goering's absence made matters worse and his influence with the Fuhrer never recovered.

31 MAY   **1942**

Herr Goering is not here of course. Of course not.

Up until that time Goering had been perhaps the greatest of the Nazi satraps. His first wife Karin had died but, when he married Emmy Sonnemann in 1935, Hitler had played a prominent part in the ceremony and told Emmy that she had become First Lady of the Third Reich. Up until the war, Goering continued as Hitler's right hand. It was he who stage-managed the *Anschluss* and he who bullied President Hacha of Czechoslovakia into agreeing the final destruction of his country. He was still high in favour after the fall of France when he was given the unique rank of Reichsmarshal—outranking Fieldmarshals—on 19 July 1940. His eclipse came only with the first failures of the Reich's war machine.

In some ways Goering's withdrawal from the centre of power has been of advantage to his post-war reputation. He was aloof from the massive extermination and slave labour programmes which characterized the New Order in its conquered territories. He even rescued a few Jews from persecution at the behest of his sympathetic wife. It would be wrong, however, to imagine that he was less of a brute than other senior Nazis. He may not have been a classic anti-semite but there are enough of his bloodthirsty statements on record to convict him of the coarsest inhumanity: 'Kill all the men in the Ukraine and then send in the SS stallions' was one, and 'This year 20-30,000,000 will die of hunger in Russia. Perhaps it is well that it should be so' just another of many.

Left: *Reichsmarshal Goering, displaying the kind of enthusiasm that was to desert him with the first failures of the Reich's war machine, but which he regained for his Nuremberg trial. From 1942 until virtually the end of the war, the Reich's highest ranking officer spent his time moving from one mansion to another, admiring his looted treasures and hunting.*

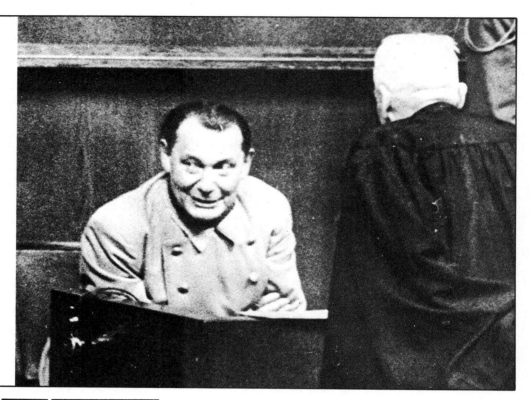

Right: *Goering on trial at Nuremberg. He was the most formidable of the defendants, shrewd and quick to score points, but it was a foregone conclusion that he would receive the death sentence—which he carried out himself, crushing a hidden cyanide capsule between his teeth.*

25 JULY   **1943**

The Reichsmarshal has been through many crises with me. He is ice cold in time of crisis. At such a time one cannot have a better adviser than the Reichsmarshal. In time of crisis the Reichsmarshal is brutal and ice cold. I have always noticed that, when it comes to the breaking point, he is a man of iron without scruples. He has been through all crises with me; through the worst crises; that is when he is ice cold. Every time it got really bad he became ice cold.

Hitler could hardly believe that Goering, who had been such a dynamo of decision up until 1942, had completely lost his taste for action. When the crisis of Mussolini's fall came, he remembered the comrade who had been such a rock in previous times of trial. It took him only 24 hours though to realize that Goering had changed: where he had been 'a man of iron without scruples' he had now become a security liability.

After that, the degeneration of the Reichsmarshal was complete. Moving from one of his vast mansions to the next he occupied his time in hunting, playing with his jewels and admiring his looted art treasures. Drugs and self-delusion kept him in a fantasy world until, in the last days of the Reich as the Fuhrer was besieged in Berlin, he took the odd notion that it was up to him to save some-

thing from the wreck. Loyal as ever he sent a message to Hitler that he would try and negotiate with the Allies. By now Hitler was half-demented and the sinister Martin Bormann convinced him that Goering's initiative was treason.

26 APRIL   **1945**

Hermann Goering has betrayed and deserted both me and his Fatherland. Behind my back he has established contact with the enemy. Now nothing remains, nothing is spared me. I immediately had Goering arrested as a traitor to the Reich.

The Gestapo arrested Goering and his family but they were released on news of Hitler's death and the chubby Reichsmarshal was able to proceed with 16 matching monogrammed suitcases of essential possessions into Allied hands.

When Goering realized that he was not to be treated as the respected envoy of an honourably defeated foe but put on trial for his life, his attitude changed. He regained something of his old energy as he made out his case at Nuremberg but it was a foregone conclusion that he would receive the death sentence. With a flicker of his old style and courage he cheated the hangman on 15 October 1946, two hours before he was due on the scaffold, by crushing a hidden cyanide capsule between his teeth.

GOEBBELS

GOEBBELS WAS THE LITTLE, CLUB-FOOTED, jug-eared scoundrel who preached the ideal of the tall, blond, blue-eyed warrior. He was malicious and absurdly lecherous but unusual among the top Nazis in possessing intelligence and not being an obvious crank or raving lunatic. When one surveys the circle of the Fuhrer's intimates and discovers such self-evident freaks as Goering, Himmler, Rosenberg or Ribbentrop, Goebbels takes on the appearance almost of conspicuous sanity.

However, a second glance shows that Goebbels had psychological problems enough. An unhandsome cripple who came from a humble background, he found his unheroic appearance galling. Worse still was the fact that he had not been fit enough to serve in World War I which so many of the Nazi comrades were able to boast of in proof of their nationalist ardour. This was a bitter blow for he felt, as did Hitler, that a man only became complete through experience of battle.

18 JANUARY   **1942**

I know how to preserve the golden mean between reason and rhetoric. In his last appeal Goebbels exhorted the soldiers at the front to remain tough and calm. I would not have expressed myself like that. In such a situation the soldier is not calm but resolved. One must have been through it to understand these matters.

To compensate for his physical inadequacy in one direction Goebbels made up for it in others. He was a really enthusiastic lover who went from one mistress's bed to the next with the greatest facility. He also had a strong desire to find a hero figure to follow and it was this desire that Hitler met. Before he encountered Hitler he was an embittered radical with a string of unsuccessful literary works behind him after his graduation from Heidelberg University. He began work for the Nazi Party in 1924 but was, initially, a follower of the socialist Gregor Strasser. A year later he was wooed by Hitler and transferred his loyalty to him.

Once Hitler was sure of Goebbels, he gave him the testing post of *gauleiter* of Berlin. The point was not only that Berlin was the capital city but that it was, in 1925, a red stronghold. In the following years, Goebbels needed endless courage and ingenuity for his struggle against the Communists and against dangerous revolts of the Berlin SA. It was to prove useful experience.

24 JUNE   **1942**

Dr. Goebbels possesses two attributes without which no one could master the conditions in Berlin—he has intelligence and the gift of oratory. I have never regretted giving him the powers he asked for.

Goebbels never let the Fuhrer down and he proved himself a campaigning journalist of genius when he launched a new newspaper *Der Angrif* (*The Attack*) in 1927. When the Party came to power in 1933 he was given his reward and made Propaganda Minister For Enlightenment.

This post was a logical progression for the man who had become the Party's master propagandist. He was the man who orchestrated the Nazi ballyhoo for each election campaign or organized impressive funerals for stormtroopers killed in brawls. When the Reichstag fire brought Hitler his golden opportunity, he found Goebbels ready to work all night to bring out a suitable propaganda blast in the next day's newspaper.

21 AUGUST   **1942**

On the night of The Reichstag fire I went to the offices of the *Volkischer Beobachter*. In the end I got hold of Goebbels and we worked till dawn preparing the next day's edition.

Being Minister for Propaganda suited Goebbels down to the ground. He was able to mount a few spectacular barbarities such as his famous book burning sessions at universities but his power extended beyond the realm of the printed word. He was also the boss of Germany's radio and movie industries. The first brought his fine resonant voice into the homes of millions of Germans which made him one of the best known Nazi leaders and the second gave him powers of patronage over scores of sexy starlets. His malicious wit and high-powered energy served him and the Party well.

The early years of the war brought the little man even greater success. His propaganda is widely credited with making a significant contribution to the fall of France, and it was easy to keep the home front happy while the news of victories rolled in. By the same token, things became progressively more difficult for the propaganda chief as failure mounted. The British had never been impressed by Goebbel's lie-dissemination machine and his British mouthpiece William Joyce (Lord Haw Haw) merely attracted delighted and incredulous laughter. By March 1942 he was made responsible for bomb damaged areas and the RAF made sure that his new responsibilities were extensive.

Worst of all though was his loss of influence with the Fuhrer. While Goebbels held the show together on the home front, Hitler was far away at his headquarters in the East absorbed in military matters. The old camaraderie was gone and Hitler was even critical in private of his loyal, hard-working Minister.

When Goebbels tried to propose any important new initiative to the Fuhrer he was always circumvented by the oafish Party Secretary Martin Bormann, who sought to consolidate his own power by excluding other influences on Hitler.

Goebbels' chance to regain power came with the Stauffenberg bomb plot of 20 July 1944. He played a key role in snuffing out the coup in Berlin and, on 26 July, he was able to prevail upon the weakened Hitler to appoint him 'Reich Trustee for Total War'. With some justification he grumbled 'If I had received these powers when I wanted them so badly, victory would be in our pockets today'. As it was, his mobilization of the entire nation for war came too late to affect the issue. On 22 April 1945 he and his wife and family joined Hitler and Eva Braun in the bunker. He was a witness to his Fuhrer's marriage and was named Chancellor in his last will and testament. But, the day after Hitler and Eva's suicide, Goebbels and his wife poisoned their children and committed suicide themselves.

Below: *Goebbels, still promoting the Nazi cause—despite falling temporarily from grace. Ultimately, he was appointed Reich Trustee for Total War, was a witness to the Fuhrer's marriage and was named Chancellor in Hitler's will.*

HIMMLER

HEINRICH HIMMLER, THE PRIM-LOOKING SON of a Bavarian schoolmaster, was the vilest of all the Nazi war criminals. It was he who controlled the dark apparatus of murder, coercion and terror that ran the Third Reich. In his hands were the Gestapo, the SS and the SD—organisations whose chilling names still evoke a ripple of disgust or fear. Yet he climbed to this pinnacle of power despite the handicap of being the most obvious crackpot that even the freak circus of the Third Reich could boast. It must have been hard work becoming a noticeable crank with Streicher, Rosenberg and Hitler himself around, and nearly impossible to compete with Goering in the conspicuous degeneracy class; but Himmler tried. That was the story of his life. He worked with continuous, clerk-like stolidity at the most mind-boggling schemes for mass murder but devoted just as much of his time and interest to weird experiments like seeing whether pepper could be grown in Germany.

Where Himmler made his mark was in bringing a lunatic approach to all aspects of life. At one moment he would assert that the preservation of the German race justified cruelty, at another he would expound on the merits of porridge and mineral water for the SS man's breakfast or raw garlic for women slave workers. With his ludicrous and most un-Nordic appearance, his outstanding crankiness and his laughable ineptitude at soldiering it is all too easy to regard Himmler as a joke—Hitler's rubber-stamp—but the reality is different. Behind the grotesque facade there was a ravening ambition that enabled him to collect one official position after another, and there was a dreadful gullibility and lack of pity about him which caused him to believe in the Nazi racial myth and to evolve its nightmare solution.

In 1927, after at least five years association with the Nazi Party, Himmler was still an obscure failure. He was an unsuccessful, unhappily-married chicken farmer with an interest in mesmerism, homoeopathy and herbal remedies—but he was also deputy leader of the SS. During a bout of opposition from the SA in 1929, Hitler made Himmler the leader of the SS (Reichsfuhrer SS) and gave him orders to make it a *corps d'elite*. In the short run, Himmler's efforts were distinctly ineffective as the mutinous SA won out against the SS. In the long run, however, he achieved what he had been asked to—he made the SS into an unquestioningly loyal unit. Looking back on it years later, Hitler paid tribute to the single-mindedness with which the object was achieved.

Opposite: *Himmler interpreted and executed Hitler's order's with real zest. His powers over life and death were limitless. Not even Stalin could later compete with his horrific extermination programme. Hitler never needed to threaten people with anything other than being 'handed over to Himmler'.*

Left: *Speaking in front of the old rallying slogan 'Germany awake', Himmler launches into another 1944 harangue. His speeches became ever more virulent as defeat approached.*

**Himmler has an extraordinary quality.
I do not believe that anyone else has had,
like him, the obligation to deploy his
troops in such constantly difficult
conditions. I see in Himmler our Ignatius
de Loyola. With intelligence and obstinacy,
against wind and tide, he formed the SS.**

Besides the SS bodyguard duties, Himmler began to accumulate police and concentration camp responsibilities. In 1933, when Hitler came to power, Himmler was made chief of the Munich police and in 1934 he became assistant chief of the Gestapo. By 1936 he had taken complete control of the SS, the SD and the Gestapo. As with so many things Himmler took up, the concentration camps which he now controlled became more 'efficient' and indeed, as the years rolled by, Hitler's joke that Himmler was becoming Germany's biggest industrialist seemed less and less unlikely.

In 1934 Himmler joined forces with Goering to despatch his immediate boss Rohm in the Night of the Long Knives. From that moment on Himmler never looked back from a career of constant acquisition of power. His was a curious empire, embracing incomparably tough and excellent soldiers along with the cold and efficient administrators of death who discussed the 'Final Solution' at working lunches. Amidst these disparate groups were the 'racial experts' with their bogus ideas about blood and soil and a new SS order of knighthood.

Even while these sinister activities occupied the Reichsfuhrer SS he found time to indulge his crankiness. He was always mustard keen on alternative medicine and particularly homoeopathy. With these preoccupations he was absolutely bound to have and encourage his own medical service. In his demented world every concentration camp had its herb garden for effecting life-saving cures, even though the prime function of some of the camps was directly opposed to such activities. Hitler, no slouch himself when it came to crackpot medical theorizing, was not at all sure about Himmler's medical schemes; they seemed to him to be a noisy fifth wheel on the coach of German medical practice.

There is no doubt that Hitler noticed that *der treue Heinrich* (honest Heinrich) was a bit odd—how could he fail to? But, with so many strange people around him, he treated the Reichsfuhrer SS with the same coarse derision that he heaped on the rest. In fact there was something sadistically comical about the alliance between Himmler's immense gullibility and his powers over life and death.

Right: *Diseased and tortured inmates in what passed as the hospital at the Buchenwald death camp.*
Opposite: *An inmate of Auschwitz dies on the wire.*

**When things at last got too hot for this
particular swindler, who claimed to be
able to extract petrol from coal with the
use of water, he tried to get a safe-conduct
out of the country. But Himmler who had
originally believed in him gave him a
carte-d'entree for one of the concentration
camps, where he was able to continue his
experiments in peace.**

Behind the comedy was a grim world that even Hitler never saw in action although he approved it. This was the world of the Death Camps in which millions of Jews and other 'undesirables' were systematically exterminated. One catches the real flavour of Himmler's character in his famous speech to SS officers at Poznan in October 1943: 'Most of you must know what it means when 100 corpses are lying side by side, or 500, or 1000', bleated the Reichsfuhrer (who could not bear executions himself) 'to have stuck it out and at the same time to have remained decent fellows, that is what has made us hard. This is a page of glory in our history'.

Though Hitler was closely interested in Himmler's extermination programme, their discussions on it were held in secret. It was Himmler's public role as merciless and loyal police chief that Hitler revelled in—to the discomfiture of his henchmen.

25 JULY · 1943

That fellow Farinacci is lucky he pulled that trick in Italy and not on me. If he had done something like that with me, I would have handed him over to Himmler immediately.

Hitler never needed to threaten people with anything other than being 'handed over to Himmler'. The knowledge that the Reichsfuhrer SS was hanging about as a bogeyman was usually enough to ensure fawning adulation—but there were times when he actually had to show his paces. His Gestapo and SS did so well on one such occasion—the unbelievably cruel execution of those involved in Stauffenberg's plot of 20 July 1944—that the Reichsfuhrer came in line for further responsibilities and honours.

He was given charge of the Replacement Army and the Volkssturm (Home Guard) and a field command was in the offing. The loutish Martin Bormann, Party Secretary and Hitler's closest confidant, was motivated entirely by the desire to destroy his rivals for Hitler's favour and he calculated that it was high time *der treue Heinrich* recorded a failure or two. 'Why not give Himmler a chance to test himself in battle?' Bormann asked Hitler, 'he will never allow Alsace to fall into American hands'. So the Reichsfuhrer was despatched to deny Alsace to the 'hopelessly Jew-ridden and Negrified' Americans. Himmler was no Napoleon and he lost it in no time at all, but Bormann's little scheme boomeranged. Hitler needed to believe in someone and he found excuses for Himmler's failure.

By now the fact that the Reich was tottering was visible even to Hitler. He was becoming worried about finding a successor to his crumbling dominion and the possibility of appointing Himmler crossed his mind but was rejected. The fellow was too inartistic—a fuhrer needed soul.

If anything happens to me, Germany will be left without a leader. I have no successor. The first, Hess, is mad; the second, Goering, has lost the sympathy of the people; and the third, Himmler, would be rejected by the Party, besides —he is so completely inartistic.

One thing Hitler was sure of was that Himmler would never betray him; he, at least, was utterly loyal. But to the Fuhrer's shocked amazement it turned out that even the Reichsfuhrer SS was not to be relied on but was caught out negotiating with the Allies. On 29 April 1945, just before he committed suicide, the Fuhrer's orders went out from the bunker that Himmler was to be stripped of all offices and dealt with.

In the end Himmler managed to avoid retribution from Hitler but, after a couple of weeks wandering about defeated Germany, fell into British hands. Once he realized that his enemies knew his identity and that they were likely to deal harshly with him, he committed suicide by biting on a cyanide capsule. Like so many of his victims, he is buried in an unmarked grave.

Below: *The clearing of the Warsaw ghetto*, 1943.

MUSSOLINI

THERE ARE CLOSE PARALLELS between the Nazi and Fascist movements and, to some extent, Hitler used Mussolini as a pattern. Certainly the two dictators made use of similar frustrations and resentments within their countries to pitch their campaign appeals.

Before World War I Mussolini had been a socialist agitator but he rejected the pacifism of his fellow socialists and was willingly conscripted in 1915. He was badly wounded in 1917 and returned from the front to find Italy sliding towards chaos. In March 1919 he formed the *Fascio di Combattimento*, a fighting party, named after the *fasces* (bundle of axe and rods) symbol of Imperial Rome. The Party began to achieve success when it campaigned against lawlessness: Mussolini called on all those who wanted the destruction of International Socialism to put on a black shirt and march in the Fascist *squadristi*. Beating up striking workers became a prime fascist activity and there were extensive disorders in 1922 as the blackshirts combatted the General Strike. By October, Mussolini ranted 'Either the government will be given to us or we will seize it by marching on Rome'. In the event, most followers of Il Duce (the Leader) were no closer than 40 miles to Rome before he was summoned to form a government.

21 JULY   **1941**

The march on Rome, in 1922, was one of the turning-points of history. The mere fact that anything of the sort could be attempted, and could succeed, gave us an impetus.

Across the Alps, Mussolini's success was watched by another nationalist agitator and demagogue. Entranced by the ease with which the Duce had grabbed power, Hitler tried his Beer-hall Putsch and failed. During the years of Hitler's continuing *Kampfzeit*, Mussolini consolidated his hold on Italy by abolishing opposition parties, the free Press and free elections. At the time of Hitler's accession to power in 1933, the Duce was established and respected, with good relations with the French and British governments. Hitler, by contrast, was regarded as dangerous and rabid—a view which Mussolini endorsed by referring to the Fuhrer as a 'mad little clown'.

The relationship between Mussolini and Hitler kicked off to an inauspicious start when the Duce crushed the new Fuhrer's hopes of a 1934 *Anschluss* by giving military guarantees to Austria. Mussolini left a conference with Hitler in June of that year claiming perceptively that he had just spoken to a madman.

'It is not difficult to govern Italy', Mussolini said, 'It is merely futile'. In a bid to add a little military excitement to the futility, he became involved in various foreign adventures. His invasion of Abyssinia (now Ethiopia) and his support for the Spanish Fascist, General Francisco Franco, put him into confrontation with the Western democracies and he began to welcome Hitler's proffered support. He announced the creation of the Rome-Berlin axis in October 1936 and the next year he visited Germany. It was this 1937 visit that decided Mussolini's future. He was awed by the titanic impression of a virile and militaristic society: the endless ranks of goose-stepping soldiers, the vast crowds hanging on the Fuhrer's words, the mighty armaments factories. From then on he threw in his lot with Hitler.

28 SEPTEMBER   **1937**

Mussolini is one of those lonely men of the ages on whom History is not tested but who themselves are the makers of History.

Hitler had always admired the Duce and made this plain. He imagined wrongly that his short, bald, lecherous Italian opposite number was turning Italy into a first-class power to march by Germany's side. In 1938, Mussolini abandoned Austria to the *Anschluss* which further cemented his relations with Germany, but emulation of the Nazis was to lead him down a perilous road.

26 AUGUST   **1939**

I am convinced that we can carry out the task imposed upon us with the military forces of Germany. I do not therefore expect to need Italy's military support in these circumstances. I also thank you, Duce, for everything you will do in future for the common cause of Fascism and National Socialism.

In May 1939 Mussolini agreed in the 'Pact of Steel' to support Germany in war. In fact, when war came, the

Duce wriggled out of his obligation but Hitler showed remarkable restraint and understanding for his ally's backsliding.

In May 1940 Hitler's remarkable series of victories over France and Britain left the Duce anxious to join in the war to claim some of the booty from an apparently beaten foe. He arranged to be made Supreme Commander of the Forces in the Field and declared war against the struggling democracies on 10 June. From the very start, the Italians found it difficult to achieve military success. The French repulsed them, the British handed them a very thorough hiding in Africa and they were humiliatingly defeated by the Greeks when they attacked them. One by one Mussolini was forced to watch the Germans take over theatres of operation in which his troops had failed. There was a dreadful corollary to this in that, in exchange for German help around the Mediterranean, Mussolini was persuaded to despatch Italian troops to help the Germans in the charnel house of the Eastern front.

I hold the Duce in high esteem because I regard him as an incomparable statesman. He is one of those who appreciated the full measure of the Bolshevik menace and, for this reason, he has sent to our Eastern front divisions of real military merit.

Opposite and below: *Mussolini, the founding father of fascism, originally spoke of Hitler as a 'mad little clown.' It was, however, a view he changed on this state visit to Germany. Awed by the endless ranks of soldiers, the vast crowds and armaments factories, he determined to emulate the Nazis and throw in his lot with Hitler.*

Hitler never lost his high opinion of Mussolini and resolutely refused to see the shortcomings of the cardboard Caesar. By mid 1942 the Italian people had been force-fed a diet of military humiliation in a conflict that they had never desired, and the Duce's popularity was beginning to wane.

24 JULY   1942

I myself have seen in a dozen different episodes in Italy how very popular the Duce is with the majority of the people.

The first intimations of this reached Hitler before Mussolini but he convinced himself that they were false. When he came to think about it later on that year, the Fuhrer realized that Mussolini had been a shade amateur about consolidating his power. Hitler was Fuhrer, Chancellor, President, Head of the Armed Forces and Commander of the Armed Forces, while the Reichstag was only assembled to provide him with suitable applause. Mere membership of the Nazi Party was considered no real guarantee of loyalty—the terror inspired by the Gestapo and SS was much more effective.

5 AUGUST   1942

The real difference between Italy and Germany is that, in the former, the Duce has not been made the Supreme Dictator of the State.

20 MAY   1943

The Duce may have the best intentions but they will be sabotaged.

Hitler mused that Italy's Head of State was the King and his position was by no means powerless, while the blackshirts of the Grand Fascist Council were not the terrified toadies of the Reichstag.

May 1943 saw the Axis surrender in North Africa and a direct threat of invasion for Sicily and mainland Italy. It was obvious to the Germans that some of their Italian allies were wavering in their loyalty to the Axis cause. Hitler had an unwavering faith in Mussolini but he was becoming increasingly concerned that the Duce was being betrayed by his followers. By 24 July 1943 the Grand

Opposite: *Mussolini reviewing a military parade of the Reich's best troops. Filled with inspiration, he returned to Italy determined to follow Hitler's example. He was shot on 28 April 1945.*

Fascist Council called on Mussolini to resign. The Duce was surprised but still indecisive: he neither resigned nor arrested his opponents. When Hitler heard the news, he was alarmed. He longed to get hold of Mussolini to put some backbone into him and urge him to take savage reprisals against his enemies.

25 JULY   1943

I am just waiting for information about what the Duce says. I want the Duce to come to Germany right away if we can get hold of him. If he will come and will talk to me that is a good sign. If he does not come, or if he is not able to get away, or if he resigns because he does not feel well—which would not surprise me with such a bunch of traitors—then one does not know.

Like a sleepwalker, Mussolini went to his political execution. On 25 July he attended an audience with the King who informed him that he was the most hated man in Italy and that he was to be replaced by Marshal Pietro Badoglio. As the ex-Duce reeled away from this painful interview he was arrested and carted off to various 'safe' spots outside Rome.

26 JULY   1943

The Duce was arrested yesterday. I do not know where the Duce himself is. As soon as I find out, I will have him brought out by paratroops.

As soon as Hitler heard the news of Mussolini's arrest he determined to rescue him. He was always extravagantly loyal to the Duce and he prepared a spectacular airborne operation. On 12 September crack German commandos rescued him from incarceration in a skiing hotel high up in the Gran Sasso mountains. The Germans helped him establish a new Fascist government in North Italy but, as the war continued, the Allies drew ever nearer, German support became weaker and the Italian people more disaffected. On 28 April 1945 Mussolini and his mistress, Claretta Petacci, were captured and shot by Italian partisans. It may be that Hitler heard of the indignities that their naked bodies were subjected to in Milan before he took his own life a few hours later—if he did it would have increased his determination that his own corpse and that of his wife should be burned to avoid that final humiliation.

THE ALLIED LEADERS

IT WAS ONLY NATURAL that a man with the kind of eccentric views that Hitler had should make enemies as well as friends. Throughout his stormy career there was resistance to him inside Germany, but it was from abroad, of course, that the strength to crush him came eventually. His limitless ambition for military conquest brought him an ally in the histrionic Italian dictator Benito Mussolini, but it made him the enemy of the three most powerful and charismatic world leaders of his era.

The first of these to enter the lists against him was the Englishman, Winston Spencer Churchill, direct descendant of that brilliant soldier the First Duke of Marlborough. Churchill had held high office in various British governments since before World War I and had been a long-time and continuous opponent of Nazism. On 10 May 1940 he became Prime Minister—just in time to preside over the disasters of the fall of France and the Dunkirk evacuation. Despite his country's apparently hopeless position, Churchill repeatedly expressed British determination to continue the war in such strong terms that Hitler came to see the dogged Prime Minister as a personal opponent.

4 MAY 1941

Churchill is the most bloodthirsty or amateurish strategist in history. For over five years he has been chasing around Europe like a madman in search of something that he could set on fire. As a soldier he is a bad politician and as a politician an equally bad soldier. The gift which Mr. Churchill possesses is the gift to lie with a pious expression on his face and to distort the truth until glorious victories are made of the most horrible defeats. His abnormal state of mind can only be explained as symptomatic of a paralytic disease or of a drunkard's ravings.

Although the Fuhrer's moods varied, he seemed to evince, in general, a grudging respect for the British people but a contemptuous fury for their leader, harping on Churchill's supposed drunkenness and on Jewish influence in his cabinet. In fact, as history shows, Churchill was a magnificent and inspiring orator, an imaginative and daring—too daring—strategist and a forceful leader. His influence and their enmity was always on Hitler's

mind and, even at the end, he continued to rail against the man who denied him his unrealistic hopes of a British alliance.

FEBRUARY 1945

If fate had granted to an ageing and enfeebled Britain a new Pitt instead of this Jew-ridden, half-American drunkard, the new Pitt would now recognize that Britain's traditional policy of balance of power would have to be applied on a world-wide scale.

Above: *This picture was used in the Nazi press to promote Hitler's view of Churchill as an elitist gangster—obsessed with continuing the war and denying England an alliance with the Reich.*

After Germany's sudden attack on Russia in 1941 Hitler came gradually to respect the dark and ruthless Josef Stalin who was, despite pretensions to Communism, the absolute ruler of that country. As the repeated hammer blows of the German Army failed to snuff out Russian resistance, a certain awe crept into Hitler's references to Stalin.

22 JULY   1942

In his own way Stalin is a hell of a fellow. He knows his models, Genghiz Khan and the rest, very well and the scope of his industrial planning is exceeded only by our own Four-Year Plan.

The continued ability of Russian forces to hit back caused Hitler some justifiable wonder at the size and strength of the Russian war machine. It must be all too true that the gigantic forces which the Germans found in Russia were originally intended to be the instrument of Stalin's own career of conquest. Stalin certainly had the necessary lack of scruple for such a course. Hitler's claim that Stalin was guilty of taking barbaric measures to preserve his state was undoubtedly true.

9 AUGUST   1942

Stalin is half beast, half giant. The people can rot for all he cares. If we had given him another ten years, Europe would have been swept away as it was in the time of the Huns.

Long before the United States entered the war against him, Hitler was conscious of the hostility of President Franklin D. Roosevelt towards National Socialism. The great American, who embodied so many of the American virtues in his vigour and idealism, was quick to realize that Hitler's regime was a threat to world stability and the rights of small nations. The Fuhrer became increasingly irritated by the President's attitude—which he regarded as an unwarrantable intrusion into European affairs. Even before the outbreak of war he was beginning to mock American attempts at mediation between himself and his intended victims with his characteristic vulgarity. He had such an extraordinarily ill-informed picture of the United States and of its President that it is easy to believe that he hoped, by a constant campaign of denigration, to convince himself that American entry into the war would matter little. In fact, following Pearl Harbour, it was Hitler and not Roosevelt who declared war.

11 DECEMBER   1941

I cannot be insulted by Roosevelt for I consider him mad. First he incites war, then falsifies the causes, then odiously wraps himself in a cloak of Christian hypocrisy and slowly but surely leads mankind to war.

In the event of the outbreak of hostilities between the Axis and the United States, Hitler was ready with a series of cheap jibes about what he imagined to be Roosevelt's role in World War I. At the last gasp of the Third Reich on 12 April 1945 President Roosevelt died and Hitler briefly indulged a hope that the Allied coalition would disintegrate as a result. In fact, American determination never wavered and the triumph which Roosevelt had sought so long was soon realized.

Above: *Franklin Delano Roosevelt, President of the United States from March 1933 until his death in April 1945. In 1932, Roosevelt had called the Presidency 'pre-eminently a place of moral leadership'—as a result of which, in his third term, he offered Britain 'All aid short of war' and made a reluctant America the 'arsenal of democracy'.*

War machine

Armaments
Armed forces

Final assembly of German naval guns.

ARMAMENTS

THERE CAN HARDLY HAVE BEEN a single German who accepted that the Treaty of Versailles in 1918 meant the end of Germany as a military power. Long before Hitler came to power, even before he became a national figure, influential German military men had secretly taken steps to flout the strict observance of Versailles. They worked on the technical side of tank construction in collusion with the Russians, and the size of the Army greatly exceeded that laid down by the Treaty because it was padded by the Secret or Black Reichswehr. The result of all this duplicity was that Hitler had some basis of technical knowledge and a large pool of trained men to assist him in building his world-conquering forces, when he began flat-out re-armament on his accession to power in the spring of 1933.

24 APRIL   **1942**

I gave instructions for the construction of the first of our new warships immediately after my assumption of power.

It was typical of Hitler and National Socialism, however, that his first action on coming to power was to give the go-ahead to symbolic gestures of rearmament. He had hardly been Chancellor more than a few days before he ordered the construction of a warship, and he was soon eagerly inspecting Germany's fledgling forces to decide on the form that their expansion should take. During a review of army units he caught his first view of the nation's embryo Panzer forces—under the command of their stoutest advocate, Heinz Guderian. Although this force was a tiny one at the time and, owing to the provisions of the Treaty of Versailles, could more properly be called a motorized rather than an armoured unit, Hitler was entranced. The impression of speed and power was completely in tune with Hitler's ideas and, as Guderian recalled, he instantly made up his mind to establish more Panzer forces. This decision was of no small importance, for the concept of Panzer units and mobile warfare was not completely accepted and had its enemies among Germany's senior soldiers. It is by no means impossible that Guderian and his sympathisers would have overcome conservative military opposition on their own, but the backing of the Chancellor and future dictator decided the issue in their favour there and then. Hitler can certainly take some of the credit for the birth and growth of the Panzers and the ideas of *Blitzkrieg*.

Yet there were more important strategic matters to concern the Fuhrer, when he contemplated war, than warships or armoured forces. Revenge for the humiliation of Versailles necessitated the defeat of France, and it was most unlikely that the French would take the field without their British allies—whose sea power posed a slow-working but deadly threat to an embattled Germany. There were some 20 basic products necessary for the manufacture of weapons and munitions and the prosecution of war in the 1930s and 1940s, and neither Germany—nor the Western Allies who were likely to oppose her—could acquire very many of them from home production. On the outbreak of war with Britain, a Naval blockade would sever Germany from foreign sources of supply, but the British armaments industry would be fed by raw materials from all parts of the globe.

During World War I Germany had shown considerable ingenuity in managing without certain materials, but the blockade had performed a powerful part in bringing her down. If Germany, as the new and virile Rome, was to escape the dreadful tentacles of the British Carthage, precautions would have to be taken to ensure that her armaments industries could obtain home based supplies.

27 JANUARY   **1942**

Vogler made me the proposal in 1933 to supply us with two million tons of synthetic petrol in the space of three years. The Ministry of Economics torpedoed the scheme.

Hitler encouraged a policy whereby artificial substitutes for such vital substances as petroleum and rubber should be manufactured from materials available within Germany. This move met much opposition from the Ministry of Economics which, sensibly, declined to see the sense in paying very much higher prices for substitutes of materials which could be bought cheaply on the world market. However, the drive for self-sufficiency or the *autarkic* economy had nothing to do with conventional economics but with rearmament. Interestingly enough, the Bank of England also pursued a 'war policy' in the 30s, by which it attempted to build up its reserves until it could finance a war for the estimated three years it would take for a blockade to work.

Opposite: *The prodigious guns of the* Scharnhorst.
Overleaf: *Hitler's Panzer units, vital to the success of* Blitzkrieg *tactics, were faced in Poland with the simple task of decimating cavalry divisions, and in Holland with routing similarly ill-equipped units.*

While the British approach arguably increased their economic difficulties, Hitler always claimed that his planned economy produced benefits for Germany.

Whatever the merits of the economic argument there is no doubt that the surge of activity wiped out the German unemployment problem. The trouble was that many German economists, including the redoubtable Schacht, believed that the pace of development was too frantic and, although they agreed with rearmament, felt that Hitler's irresponsibility would strain the economy. In the event, the coming of war meant that the argument was never resolved.

Rearmament was inseparable from National Socialism. In pursuit of his ideals Hitler's sole purpose was to transfer Germany into the position of a great power again and, as was not apparent to everyone, to actually fight and win a major war. When he embarked on this course in 1933 he was forced to dissemble.

12 NOVEMBER   **1933**

My Party comrades will not fail to understand me when they hear me speak of universal peace, disarmament and mutual security pacts.

The French might be uncertain of themselves but they enjoyed, temporarily, much greater military power than Germany. Until the programme of rearmament was advanced it was better to mask Nazi intentions with fair words. As Hitler realized, nobody in Germany could have any doubts about his ultimate intentions, but his future victims could easily be bluffed.

The frantic speed of rearmament soon meant that attempts to maintain secrecy were an unnecessary brake and, in 1935, Hitler found an excuse to repudiate publicly the provisions of Versailles. Once the wraps were off, Hitler's urgency again proved dangerous to an orderly programme of expansion for the Armed Forces. He arbitrarily fixed the size of his new conscript army at 36 divisions in the first place, although his generals had estimated that 21 divisions would be a desirable maximum as the 4,000 officers of the existing army could not cope with training requirements much beyond that. From this time on, the Fuhrer became accustomed to riding rough-shod over any bleating about difficulties from his General Staff by insisting that the dynamism of the Nazi movement could prevail over any obstacles. To some extent he was right, in that he was merely seeking to arm and train a society which had already been made highly militaristic.

As Hitler well knew, the decision to rearm was more easily taken in a dictatorship and it would not be simple to persuade people in the Western democracies that war was inevitable. He gloated over the growing military advantage that this would bring him as each year passed.

24 OCTOBER   **1936**

German and Italian rearmament is proceeding much more rapidly than rearmament can in Great Britain where it is not only a case of producing ships, guns and aeroplanes but also of undertaking psychological rearmament. In three years Germany will be ready, in four years more than ready; if five years are given, better still.

The main point about the new war machine that Hitler was constructing was that it also had a vital qualitative superiority over its opponents. This was, oddly enough, not absolute in the standard of weapons that it disposed of but in the method which it chose for making war— *Blitzkrieg*. The idea of the lightning war revolved around deep and rapid penetration of an enemy's position by armoured and motorized forces. In the event, it proved successful because of the superiority of the Luftwaffe in ground support and the ability of self-contained Panzer divisions to manoeuvre with great speed and a measure of independence from the slower moving army units. Obviously this radically new type of force needed a lot of the most modern war materials such as trucks, tanks, wireless units and mobile artillery. Before the war and during the first couple of years of it, while the Panzer units and the Luftwaffe were high in Hitler's favour, Germany's war production was more or less successfully bent to provide for them. As time passed, it became clear that Hitler had no real conception of the sort of weaponry which was required by a war of manoeuvre and, because he was the fountain of all power in the Third Reich, his interference in the planning and production of weaponry was to have fatal consequences for the German Armed Forces.

26 AUGUST   **1939**

If there should be a war I shall build U-boats, I shall build aeroplanes and annihilate my enemies.

It is apparent that the Fuhrer only backed the production of the modern weapons which gave his forces such a decisive edge from 1939-42 because they seemed to him to be weapons of terror. He harped incessantly on the things he knew his enemies feared—bombers that would flatten their cities, U-boats that would destroy their trade and starve them into submission. It was, no doubt, the dread which tanks inspired which caused him to increase their number. Once built, they proved themselves so thoroughly in peacetime manoeuvres that most German senior soldiers were won over by them. The trouble was that the Fuhrer himself, an ex-World War I corporal, had no real conception of their role.

16 AUGUST   **1942**

Before the war, when I saw that the Army could not be induced to take any steps as regards motorization, I went myself to Krupps and arranged that the SS units should be equipped with Panzer Mark IV.

The story of Germany's mechanization of her forces, as Hitler told it, was that he was the far-seeing genius who had first seen its advantages and convinced the generals. What is more, he gave himself the credit for ordering, from Krupps, a generous allocation of Panzer Mark IV, which served as the Army's nearest approximation to a main battle tank until the introduction of the Panther in July 1943. In fact the Mark IV was very sparsely distributed among Panzer and SS Panzer forces until after the success of the 1940 campaign against France.

The early campaigns showed up the various defects of the German tank force—much is often made of the fact that the French had more tanks which were, in some respects, better. The chief defects were to do with gun calibration, for the tanks used in 1939 and 1940 did not show as much ability to penetrate enemy armour as was desired. Calibration was a simply explained technical equation to do with the kinetic energy imparted to shot, and Hitler understood it. He was sympathetic to his generals' requests and happy to press for the upgunning of their tanks, but it was quite obvious that the purpose of armoured forces escaped him, even while they were producing the amazing successes with which they began the Russian campaign.

29 OCTOBER   **1941**

We should keep motorization within reasonable limits. In the choice between mobility and power, the choice in peace time is too often given in favour of mobility. At the end of World War I, experience had shown that only the heaviest and most thickly armoured tank had any value.

Hitler could not see that it was the motorization of his forces rather than the power of their armour which enabled them to achieve their victories. The potency of the Panzers lay in the back-up, from motor lorries to mobile workshops, which gave them their ability to out-manoeuvre the enemy. Yet Hitler in October 1941 was expressing an opinion that, in extension, would have resulted in the production of the German equivalent of British Infantry (I) tanks—ponderous eight mile an hour leviathans with almost impermeable front armour and a hopeless record against General Erwin Rommel's faster moving Panzer III and IV.

The German Army received a few nasty shocks in Russia and, among them, was the discovery of the Russian T34 tank which could only be knocked out by expertly directed shots from the 50mm calibre gun of the Panzer Mark III. This was a problem which Hitler's magpie mind could easily comprehend, and such ideas of tank construction as he had were soon dominated by considerations of armour thickness and gun power to the exclusion of manoeuvrability and facility of production. The most ludicrous result of this was the celebrated *maus* project—by which 189-ton prototypes were being tested by the end of the war. Lesser aberrations were the Tiger and Royal Tiger tanks which put the fear of God into their opponents but which were too few in number (and, in the case of the Royal Tiger, under-engined) to effect the fast-moving, deep-penetration role of the truly effective armoured force. In addition to this, each Royal Tiger used up the manufacturing resources of two Panther tanks.

The Panther, which is usually regarded as the finest main battle tank of the war, owed little to Hitler. Its specifications were decided upon by a committee of enquiry appointed by Guderian. If the 8,000,000 men that Hitler had under arms in 1944 had been adequately provided with Panthers, there would have been a real possibility that the war might have gone the other way. However, just as the German firm of MAN (Maschinenfabrik-Ausgburg-Nurnberg) were developing its prototype in 1942, Hitler was convincing himself that the tank had had its day.

4 JANUARY   **1942**

The hollow charge means the death of the tank. With the help of this weapon, anyone at all can blow up a tank. When the Russians start up again in the spring their tanks will be put out of action.

Hitler's belief that it was the turn of the anti-tank projectile was enough latitude for his brilliant armaments Minister Speer to adopt, in large measure, the cheaper alternative of producing a turretless, anti-tank AFV in preference to the genuine article. All this brainwork by the Fuhrer with his preference for over-gunned, over-armoured, over-weight tanks or turretless tank killers had a very restrictive effect on tank production. During the war, Germany hardly managed to equal the tank production record of bombed and disrupted British industry —it was several hundred per cent lower than Russian or US production. With the war's best main battle tank and an army and commanders best able to use it, Germany's efforts were practically sabotaged by the Fuhrer's quirky misunderstandings and dogmatic assertions on warfare.

Things were little better for the Navy, although it was a while before Hitler got into full stride in interfering with ship construction. The Navy's early mistakes, such as making their pocket battleships too lightly armoured (for the sake of speed), were all their own. However, when the Fuhrer felt in world-conquering mood even the intricacies of ordering a completely new design of naval vessel were not beyond him.

2 JUNE   1942

I can only hope that our Naval experts will at last allow themselves to be persuaded that their method of ship construction is out of date. I have ordered that the Sachsen ship, with its motive power in front, should immediately be built and given tests. I have further directed that tests be made of the practicability of propelling a ship by means of lateral screws—after the manner of a fish's fins.

The German Navy had begun to produce such a success story by 1942 that even Hitler could hardly ignore it. The weapon which proved so effective was the U-boat, an old favourite, but Hitler's lack of interest in Naval affairs was so profound that he had failed to allocate more than the most meagre resources even to U-boat construction. By July 1942 he saw the light, and his U-boats came nearer to defeating Britain and baffling America than ten times the investment in other weaponry could have done. In the end the U-boats failed, and that might just possibly have been because it took until 1942 for Hitler to see that the possession of technical superiority at sea was the key to success. As far as the surface fleet was concerned, Hitler was not above a dramatic gesture. On New Year's Day 1943 he became carried away in a tirade on its uselessness and ordered that it be decommissioned and broken up for scrap. This was too much for Admiral Raeder who resigned, to be succeeded by the U-boat expert Admiral Doenitz.

Rages about naval failures were as nothing to rages about the defects of the Luftwaffe. The pre-war build up of Germany's Air Force had been left to Hermann Goering—a moderately sensible choice of Nazi leader considering that Goering had been the last commander of the famous Richthofen Circus in World War I. Goering was, at base, an idle man and some of his old wartime comrades, whom he appointed to assist him, were not much better. They had the advantage of combat experience which enabled them to appreciate the qualities of the aircraft that they produced; but they did not have the

Below and opposite: *Britain came perilously close to losing what would have been the most decisive battle of the war—the Battle of the Atlantic. In the end the U-boats failed, perhaps because it took until 1942 for Hitler to see the importance of technical superiority at sea.*

organizational flair to ensure a satisfactory level of production. Undoubtedly their knowledge led to the early successes of the Luftwaffe, and their slackness to its eclipse.

While things went well Hitler did not question the Luftwaffe's effectiveness and he made little attempt to exercise his 'genius' on aircraft construction. Even the comparative failure of the Battle of Britain did not arouse him, because the struggle with Britain had not been pressed *à outrance*. At the beginning of 1942, he was still ignorantly boastful of the superior qualities of German aircraft and obviously being misled by Goering and the Luftwaffe commanders.

17 JANUARY   **1942**

Recently one of our new Messerschmitts fell into enemy hands. They were dumbfounded. It was necessary for them to yield to the evidence that, within three years at least, the United States would not be able to produce an aircraft of that quality. It must be observed that a German aircraft requires at least six times as much work as an American aircraft.

When Hitler said that German aircraft were six times as difficult to produce as American aircraft because of their superior quality, it is evident that he was ingenuously rehearsing excuses which had been made to him by the men responsible for the Luftwaffe's dismal productivity record. Within months the American Air Forces would prove to him that they produced fighters and bombers which were superior in quantity and quality to anything in German hands.

Although Hitler was a great enthusiast for handing out destruction to the Reich's enemies, he was markedly less keen when destruction was visited by them upon Germany. He talked glibly and callously of razing London or totally destroying Moscow and Leningrad by bombing, but finally realized at the beginning of 1942 that these desirable objectives had not been obtained by the Luftwaffe. Indeed it was filtering through to him that the citizens of the Reich, far to the west of his military headquarters, were having to sustain casualties and damage from a growing RAF bomber offensive. Steps would have to be taken and it was a happy coincidence that the superiority of German technology would enable

Below: *A formation of Stukas.*
Opposite: *A Stuka releases its bombs after a near vertical dive. It was not an elegant plane, but deliberately designed for mass production. Allied fighters eventually demonstrated how vulnerable it was.*

the Third Reich to make the proper riposte. The development of jets would give the Germans a decisive edge over the Allies.

The jet would lend itself to the protection of Germany by powering matchless fighters to knock down all the bombers the Allies could put into the sky. When the excited Luftwaffe bosses presented Hitler with this dazzling opportunity they were dismayed to find that his mind had been working differently.

9 FEBRUARY   **1942**

If I had a bomber capable of flying at more than 750 kilometers per hour, I would have supremacy everywhere. This aircraft would not have to be armed for it would be faster than the fastest fighters. In our manufacturing schedules we should first tackle the problem of bombers instead of giving priority to fighters, where production can catch up quickly.

Above: *An ME 110 over the Channel.*
Opposite: *The gun camera of a US F-51 Mustang caught this German jet-propelled Messerschmitt 262, seconds before the Mustang destroyed it. The action took place over Germany during a raid by heavy bombers of the 8th Air Force on oil targets. Hitler's interference in the jet programme caused lasting harm to the German war effort.*

The Fuhrer intended to defend Germany not by producing a fighter defence but by bombing his enemies into submission. His lust for the offensive was undimmed (as befitted a man who liked to relax by watching film of London burning at the height of the Blitz) and he regarded fighters as a negative, defensive solution. His order went out that the jet should be developed as a bomber. Goering was not a man to disobey the Fuhrer and so he urged his technical experts to begin adaptation. Once more Hitler's misinformed opinions had done lasting harm to the war effort by bringing about a total misuse of a revolutionary new aeroplane and causing long and unnecessary delays in its production. Having achieved all this disruption, however, Hitler still expected great things from his jets.

3 JUNE   1942

**In war the soldier who achieves the
greatest success is the one who has the
most modern technical means at his
disposal.**

Hitler was intoxicated by technology, and he repeatedly remarked on the decisive advantage which accrued to the side which held a lead in technical accomplishment. This particular facet of his character was the one which brought the most harm to the German war machine. The trouble was that he believed that he himself possessed technical qualifications, which he did not, and he was as unwilling to accept the advice of scientifically trained advisers as he was to listen to military advice from his soldiers. He was absurdly dogmatic and irrational in argument—maintaining the overriding attitude that he was an intuitive genius who knew best.

With this unique gift for truly damaging interference in armament programmes, Hitler coupled a strong streak of willful self-delusion. He consistently derided American soldiers and equipment because he did not want to believe in their effectiveness. He refused to concede that the figures he was given for Russian tank production were true because he did not want to believe that they were true. In the same way he pinned ludicrously high hopes on any slight advantages that he might be able to command. One of these advantages was the jet and, despite all he had done to sabotage it, he seemed to believe that the appearance of a few jets would be enough to repel the Anglo-American assault on Europe.

20 DECEMBER   1943

**We are hoping that our new planes will
arrive before the enemy attacks (in the
West). Every moment we delay that
attack improves our situation. With each
month the likelihood increases that we
will get a group of jet fighters.**

In the event, the jets caused a ripple of alarm when they eventually appeared but, by then, the war was lost and the Allied air superiority was so overwhelming that nothing could shake it—particularly as German factories were under constant attack.

With Hitler's belief in his technical qualifications went a fascination for irrelevant detail. All sorts of ideas, many of them misconceived, racketed about inside his head and he was never short of a quickfire opinion on any technical

topic. It was disturbing for his soldiers to find the man who had made himself their overall commander absorbing himself in matters like the grade of lubricating oil to be used in military automotives during the Russian winter. The worst aspect of this fitful interest was that it was likely to lead to instructions based on illogical prejudice, which were nevertheless instructions that had to be obeyed or laboriously circumvented.

28 AUGUST   1942

**The best AA gun is the 88. The 105 has the
disadvantage that it consumes too much
ammunition and the life of the barrel is
very short. The double-barrelled 128 has
a fantastic appearance. When one
examines the 88 with the eye of a
technician, one realizes that it is the
most beautiful weapon yet fashioned,
with the exception of the 128.**

It was ruinously irresponsible for a man of Hitler's limitations to be involved in any equipment specifications except in the role of rubber stamp to better informed recommendations. Yet no aspect of the war was safe from him. He had no objective basis for any of his judgements but was happy to make dogmatic statements about the relative virtues of AA guns with glib facility and even claim that he examined them 'with the eye of a technician'.

12 AUGUST   1942

**In the future, small arms must consist
of machine-guns and automatic rifles
only. Every weapon must have a telescopic
site if accuracy is to be deadly.**

It was also difficult to judge how seriously Hitler's opinion was meant to be taken. When he held forth that small arms were all to have a fully automatic loading system, he was obviously quite ignorant of the difficulties of ammunition supply which would result in the field. His insistence that these weapons should have telescopic sights showed that he had no grasp of the realities of industrial production since there was no way that any significant quantity of telescopic sights could have been provided by Axis manufacturers; it also showed that he had no insight to the problems of combat—given a mass of targets at ranges of 200 metres or less, telescopic sights would actually slow down the soldiers' ability to locate each new target. In fact these ideas on small arms were just tossed off by the thoughtless Fuhrer allowing free rein to

Left: *An underground V2 production line at Nordhausen, Germany. 4000 V2s were launched: 1504 landed on England, killing 2700 people and injuring 6250.*

Below: *This photograph was taken from a Fleet Street roof-top in London; the bomb exploded in a side road.*

his supposedly unrivalled intuition in military matters. They were not pressed on suffering infantry commanders or demanded from over-extended German industry—but they could have been. Hitler's combination of absolute power, complete self-confidence and a quirky fascination with the easily assimilable parts of technical problems meant that the German war effort was never safe from incompetent interference.

Where science became more abstruse, so that Hitler could make no pretence to understand its details, he had, perforce, to refrain from meddling. In this area his trouble was that his love of the absolute made him exaggerate the significance of technical advance. Because they were incomprehensible to him and represented a new generation of military hardware, he regarded the V-1 and V-2 rockets with which he intended to pound London as something akin to the last trump.

The British should be nervous of his rockets, he felt—he knew that they could destroy Berlin, or so he thought, if they were in Allied hands. To some extent his bewilderment at the progression of his arsenal must have been reflected in the West. The real feelings of Churchill, Roosevelt and Truman about the atom bomb project must have been a mixture of disbelief and apprehension—it was all such a long way from the light tanks and bombers of 1939.

28 DECEMBER   **1944**

The enemy has full knowledge of the flying bombs. Just as we are causing continual disturbances to the English industrial regions through these flying bombs, so the enemy will be able to demolish the Ruhr area by the mass shooting of flying bombs.

In Hitler, the counterpart of exultation at the advantage the rockets gave him was the fear of what would happen when the Allies, with their superior industrial resources, began to develop them.

Towards the end of the war, when German industrial capacity had been totally incapacitated by air attack or overrun by ground troops, there had been a vast and undeniable advance in the weapons of destruction. German technology had been at least equal to the challenge: chasing British radar superiority, trying its own atom bomb programme, dreaming up the V rockets and keeping a constantly high standard of construction in aircraft, conventional weapons and vehicles. It was in production that the Germans failed and this failure was in some sense due to Hitler's own failings in comprehension and humility.

29 APRIL   **1945**

I have made too many offers for the control and limitation of armaments for the responsibility for the outbreak of this war to be laid on me.

As a final gesture to add insult to injury the Fuhrer had the gall to maintain that he was not really a weapons enthusiast at all. It was all a monstrous injustice that people should accuse him of being keen on rearming or going to war.

Below: *Mobile gun stations were the only answer to Allied air superiority. This particular gun could fire 300 kilogram shells. By the end of the war, when German industry had been totally incapacitated by air attack, there had been a vast and undeniable advance in such weapons of destruction.*

ARMED FORCES

THERE WERE A NUMBER OF SUBJECTS which cropped up in Hitler's conversation again and again. His stale repetition of the days of *Kampfzeit* or happy times on the Obersalzberg was varied only by continual reference to his life as a soldier in World War I. These were the formative periods of his life, the times when he had been happy.

13 OCTOBER   **1941**

> **The only period when I had no worries was the six years of life as a soldier . . . After that the worries came back.**

For a man of Hitler's tastes the period of army life with its lack of personal responsibility and its feeling of belonging to a gigantic, purposeful movement was a treasured memory. Although his opinion of the organization of the German war machine in World War I varied, he generally referred to the Army itself with pride and admiration. When he left the Army he was a committed militarist and he was, to some extent, sponsored as a nationalist demagogue by the military command in Bavaria. He was, at that time, very much the Army's creature and proud of it.

Even as the Nazi Party began to gain significance, Hitler was anxious to show himself the obedient servant of military interests. The failure of his Beer-hall Putsch had made him wary of taking on the established forces of the state and he determinedly wooed the generals—who were not displeased by his emphasis on rearmament. Although the temptation to seize power by revolution increased with the strength of the Party and, in particular, its partially armed military wing the SA, Hitler held his hand.

As Hitler explained later, he could not rely on the sympathy of the Army officer corps. If he tried a revolution, the Army could make it an excuse for a power bid of its own. Besides, Hitler was sure that once he was established and could re-introduce conscription, the recruits flowing into the Army would be strongly influenced by National Socialism and so the generals could no longer rely on their absolute loyalty if they should decide to take action against him. Once he was firmly in the saddle, the Army would find that its sting had been drawn.

So, although there was a certain amount of mutual suspicion, neither Hitler nor the officer caste were actually antagonistic when Hitler came to power. The generals were delighted with the rearmament programme which was swiftly unveiled, and the Fuhrer himself had no wish to destroy an institution which he still regarded as an admirable one. As he was to show during the Night of the Long Knives he did not wish to change the Army's character but simply to expand and strengthen it—to make it great again.

21 MAY   **1942**

> **My decision to attain power constitutionally was influenced primarily by my knowledge of the attitude of the Wehrmacht towards the Chancellorship. If I had siezed power illegally the Wehrmacht would have constituted a dangerous breeding place for a coup d'état. By acting legally I was in a position to restrict the Wehrmacht to its legal and strictly limited military functions—at least until such time as I was able to introduce conscription. After that, the influx into the Wehrmacht of the masses of the people, together with the spirit of National Socialism and the power of the National Socialist Movement, would, I was sure, enable me to overcome all opposition within the armed forces, and in particular the corps of officers.**

It was with some irritation that Hitler found that the Army did not seem to be as dedicated to its own revival as he was. The generals persisted in finding obstacles to his headlong rush for military power. At the re-introduction of conscription there was the first hint of the level-headed approach which was to infuriate the Fuhrer and which he was to castigate as lack of enthusiasm or worse. Its commanders had asked for the Army to be increased to a total of 21 divisions and estimated that the 4,000 officers of the existing Army could not cope with an increase beyond a maximum 24 divisions. On 16 March 1935, when Hitler announced the abrogation of the Treaty of Versailles and the expansion of the Army, he arbitrarily fixed its new size at 36 divisions.

16 AUGUST   **1942**

> **Even with good old Fritsch I had a battle royal on the day I re-introduced conscription.**

As he recalled the incident later, Hitler was inclined to

regard it with geniality and still referred to the general who was then Commander in Chief of the Army as 'good old Fritsch', but there is no doubt that it caused a certain ill feeling. Hitler was not pleased with the Army's feebleness and the Army was unhappy when it realized that Hitler had got his own way despite military advice—the German officer corps was not used to being disregarded.

The temporary hiccup in the cordial relationship between Fuhrer and his senior soldiers was soon smoothed over as all parties were exhilarated by the idea of rearmament. The German Army had always had an important part in society—it had virtually ruled the country during World War I—and it enjoyed enormous respect and affection from the German people: to them it was almost the symbol of national existence. Hitler was as affected by this attitude of worship of the military as anyone, and it was a matter of pride to him that he had been instrumental in the revival of such a favoured institution.

16 SEPTEMBER 1935

It is the Army which has made men of us all and when we looked upon the Army our faith in the future of our people was always reinforced. This old glorious Army is not dead; it only slept, and now it has risen again.

At this stage Hitler was still full of enthusiasm for the Army and gratitude to it—it was the school which would build the nation anew and serve to achieve the mounting ambitions of its Fuhrer.

The rearmament programme was not restricted to the Army alone. On 9 March 1935 the Allied governments had officially been informed that the Luftwaffe was in existence and, that June, Ribbentrop brought off the coup of the Anglo-German Naval Treaty which allowed Germany to build up to 35 per cent of British strength in surface ships and 100 per cent in submarines. There is no doubt that the progress of these two armed services gave Hitler great satisfaction but, for certain reasons, he was able to avoid the close personal involvement with them that was to characterize his relationship with the Army. He was always sure that the Navy and the Luftwaffe were in good National Socialist hands. The Luftwaffe was commanded by Goering and had never had a history independent of National Socialism. The Navy was not so strong on tradition as the Army and the admirals whom Hitler appointed as its commanders were 100 per cent Nazis.

The commanders of the Army had not been appointed by Hitler and he soon had cause to doubt the fervour of their commitment to Nazism. As he was gradually to

Below: *Hitler and the leaders of his new* Wehrmacht *watch a march past. From left to right: Colonel General Hermann Goering (Luftwaffe), Fieldmarshal Werner von Blomberg (War Minister and Wehrmacht C-in-C), Colonel General Baron von Fritsch (Army), Admiral Erich Raeder (Navy) and colleague, General Ritter von Leeb.*

discover, the *esprit* of the old Prussian General Staff survived throughout the officer corps. He could find plenty of Nazi sympathisers in its ranks but, even among them, their professional training tended to keep them aloof from the unquestioning acceptance of his will which was what he required. In fact he appears to have achieved his smoothest working relationship with the group of senior commanders whose appointments preceded or coincided with his rise to power. The senior serving soldier at this time was Fieldmarshal Werner von Blomberg, who was in the cabinet as War Minister and who was, in addition, Commander in Chief of the German Armed Forces. Blomberg was so compliant with Hitler's wishes that he was mockingly christened the 'rubber lion' by less committed brother officers. The Commander in Chief of the Army was 'good old Fritsch', General Werner von Fritsch. Although the Fuhrer's relationship with these two was relatively cordial, they were both to be broken in an extraordinary crisis involving their sexual conduct in 1938.

The slight irritation which Hitler felt towards Blomberg and Fritsch was increased by the events which followed his decision to reoccupy the Rhineland—which had been demilitarized by the Treaty of Versailles.

Below: *Fieldmarshal Rommel, was given charge of the Atlantic Wall. Ordered to make the French coast impregnable, he almost succeeded—but made the wrong guess as to the most likely Allied invasion sector.*

27 JANUARY 1942

What would have happened on 13 March 1936 if anyone but myself had been at the head of the Reich? I threatened, unless the situation eased in 24 hours, to send six extra divisions into the Rhineland. The fact was that I had only four brigades.

The generals were only too aware that the operation carried a grave military risk as it could only be carried out by insignificant forces, Germany's rearmament had not, by then, advanced far. Hitler was contemptuous of their fears and later compared them with his own aplomb in bluffing his way through the crisis. In this was the beginning of the constantly reiterated claim that the Fuhrer was always right and the timid generals often wrong.

In November 1937 Hitler warned the Army to prepare for action against Austria and Czechoslovakia and stated that he was prepared to risk war with the Western powers. Blomberg and Fritsch were naturally anxious about this and Fritsch even had the temerity to warn the Fuhrer against such a suicidal course. While these two senior soldiers were low in Hitler's esteem as a result of such faint-heartedness, they were framed and disgraced in a conspiracy which was probably organized by Goering and Himmler.

Blomberg was a widower who was considering marrying his secretary. This would have been a slight *mesalliance* by the strict standards of the officer corps, but Goering encouraged the wretched 'rubber lion' and even shipped off a rival for the young lady's affections to South America. The 60-year-old Fieldmarshal married his secretary, Fraulein Gruhn, on 12 January 1938. On 25 January, Goering brought the Fuhrer startling evidence that Blomberg's new wife was a prostitute with an extensive history with the German police. There were even salacious photographs of the new Frau Fieldmarshal in pornographic poses. Blomberg was forced to resign but, before he left for an extended honeymoon on Capri to console himself with the arts which his new wife had learned in a Berlin massage parlour, he was given a word of encouragement by Hitler.

25 JANUARY 1938

As soon as Germany's hour comes, Blomberg will again be by my side and everything that has happened in the past will be forgotten.

As far as is known, Hitler told Blomberg that he would be recalled to the supreme command in the event of war. This promise was never fulfilled.

At that moment, Himmler's Gestapo were moving against Fritsch. They produced a dossier which allegedly proved that Fritsch was a homosexual susceptible to blackmail. When Fritsch protested his innocence, the Gestapo produced a degenerate called Hans Schmidt who claimed to have seen the Army chief committing an unnatural act with a certain 'Bavarian Joe' in a dark corner near Potsdam railway station. Although Fritsch was later found innocent of this ludicrously clumsy frame-up, he was relieved of his command 'for health reasons' on 4 February.

Before there could be much speculation as to who should succeed the fallen warriors, Hitler came up with a novel scheme for their replacement.

4 FEBRUARY   **1938**

From now on I take over personally the command of the whole armed forces.

Hitler himself took over Blomberg's position as commander in chief of all three services and he re-organized the institutions of command. Instead of a War Ministry, he presided over the Supreme Command of the Armed Forces—*Oberkommando der Wehrmacht* (OKW) which was a new creation. To assist him in managing the nation's armed forces he chose the pliant General Wilhelm Keitel and gave him the imposing title of Chief of the Supreme Command of the Armed Forces. His team was completed by the appointment of General Alfred Jodl as the Operations Chief of the OKW—a post which Jodl held throughout the war.

While Hitler was snugly fitted up as Supreme Commander of all the armed services, he also had to make arrangements to find an Army commander and establish him in a separate headquarters. The Army High Command was known as the *Oberkommando des Heeres* (OKH) and, in accordance with the weight of German tradition, the executive commander of this office would be hardly more important than the Chief of the German General Staff who would also occupy it. Hitler made General (later Fieldmarshal) Walter von Brauchitsch Commander in Chief of the Army and inherited the unbending General Ludwig Beck as Chief of the German General Staff. During this reshuffle 16 senior generals were dismissed and 44 others transferred. Beck, who was a stern traditionalist, was ill-prepared to put up with this high handed approach and, when he found that Hitler had designs on Czechoslovakia, he resigned to be succeeded in August 1938 by his deputy, General Franz Halder.

So, as war approached, the Germans soldiered on

towards it with a rather ambiguous command structure. Although the employment of land forces would, in the past, have automatically involved the German General Staff and, if only for form's sake, the Commander in Chief of the Army, this would no longer be the case now that ex-corporal Hitler was possessed of a military staff and a certain title to interfere. Although the Polish campaign was organized by the Army in orthodox fashion, it was succeeded by considerable dissention between OKW and OKH. Hitler wanted immediate action in the West in the autumn of 1939 but, for various reasons, the professional soldiers of OKH dragged their feet and told him that the timing was not propitious.

While the generals at OKH busied themselves with delaying the assault on the West, Hitler laid very secret plans for the invasion of Denmark and Norway. OKW had some title to be in charge of this operation because it would involve the Navy and the Luftwaffe as well as the Army, but the Fuhrer's senior soldiers were stunned at not being consulted. They knew nothing of the proposed operations until General Falkenhorst, Hitler's appointed commander, called on them to demand that they make five divisions available to him. As Halder noted indignantly on 26 February 'Not a single word on this matter has been exchanged between the Fuhrer and Brauchitsch'.

On 9 April the operation, masterminded by the Fuhrer and OKW, commenced and, despite a great deal of success, might have failed in its eventual objectives if the stunning blows of May 1940 in France had not forced the British and French to abandon the Norwegians.

The attack on Holland, Belgium and France could hardly be undertaken without involving the Army chiefs but their freedom of action was constricted by interference from Hitler at OKW. The famous order to stop the Panzers on the Aa canal on 24 May stemmed from OKW and was given by Hitler. As a result of this blunder the British Expeditionary Force was able to escape at Dunkirk—although, at the time, the significance of this was not appreciated. In the aftermath of the fall of France, relations between Hitler and his soldiers were so good that he made 12 generals into Fieldmarshals on 19 July. Nine of them were Army generals, but Halder—Chief of the German General Staff—was not given the coveted baton. Hitler was not fond of Halder.

The attack on Russia in 1941 was a mirror of that on France in the jostling of OKH by OKW. Forces were switched hither and thither at Hitler's behest and real acrimony between him and his commanders began to grow as the battle began to go against them. In response to the wave of counter-attacks in the cruel winter weather, Brauchitsch considered it his duty to extricate the Army from the heart of Russia.

19 DECEMBER   **1941**

This little matter of operational command is something anyone can do. The task of the Commander in Chief of the Army is to train the Army in a National Socialist way. I know of no general who could do that as I want it done. Consequently I have decided to take over command of the Army myself.

Hitler was determined to hang on to every inch of ground and the disagreement was resolved when Brauchitsch offered to resign on 17 December. To Halder's astonishment, Hitler decided to take over Brauchitsch's functions himself, making no effort to conceal the fact that he considered the Commander in Chief of the German Army played a very undemanding role. More important than this, however, was Hitler's outspoken belief that the timidness and lack of willpower of the officer corps had prevented him from gaining a victory. The National Socialist virtue of morale was all that Hitler looked for. Any failure was to be attributed to weakness, and during that winter many generals were broken and one even sentenced to death for ordering tactical retreats.

From the point of view of the prestige of Germany's military establishment, Hitler's success in the winter of

Above: *The only picture published of an Enigma machine in use. General Guderian's cipher clerk puzzles over a signal to be enciphered for radio transmission. Churchill referred to Enigma as 'my most secret source'; the Allies possession of one of the machines was undoubtedly the best-kept secret of the war.*

1941-42 was a disaster. His untutored determination to make an unyielding stand has often been acknowledged as the only thing that saved the German Army from the rout that might have resulted from retreat. From this time on, the Fuhrer was convinced that his grasp of military and strategic matters was superior to that of his generals and he was unwilling to put up with any of their arguments. Worse than this for the future suffering of German soldiers was his conviction that anything could be achieved through blind dedication and sacrifice.

6 JANUARY   **1942**

If Brauchitsch had remained at his post, even if only for another few weeks, the matter would have ended in catastrophe. He is no soldier, he is but a poor thing and a man of straw.

Ever afterwards Hitler referred to the retired Brauchitsch with contempt. Like all the 'gentlemen' who wrote von in front of their names he had not got the hardness and resolve which was what Nazi generalship was all about. To Hitler he was a 'man of straw' whose lack of belief had jeopardized the Army. Whereas he had been restrained by the point of view of professional soldiers before this, he was now prepared to overrule them or dismiss them at the first sign of opposition.

During the first eight months of 1942 Hitler still suffered the restraint of having Halder as Chief of the General Staff. In some respects Halder's appointment had been a departure from the traditions of the General Staff in that he was a Catholic by religion and hailed from southern Germany. However, Halder possessed all the usual virtues of the professional staff officer and he was able to balance Hitler's undoubted gifts for over-all strategy with the details of operational planning. While he

Below: 30 *January 1943, Hitler plots the next move in the disastrous Russian campaign.*

was still at OKH the longstanding and efficient German military system was still in some sort of working order. As time went by the friction which was always bound to occur between the megalomaniac Fuhrer who believed that he was an infallible military genius and the trained soldier who was responsible for giving effect to his orders became unbearable. Halder and every other senior soldier in the German Army could see the situation around Stalingrad worsening in the autumn of 1942. There was absolutely no reason for the German Army to sustain a defeat when a simple withdrawal might even put it in the position of achieving a tactical victory. Repeated hammering at this point was agony for Halder as it was infuriating for Hitler.

24 SEPTEMBER　　　　　　　　　　　　　　　**1942**

> **Halder is no longer equal to the psychic demands of his position. He and I have been suffering from nerves. Half my nervous exhaustion is due to him. It is not worth going on. We need National Socialist ardour now not professional ability. I cannot expect this of an officer of the old school such as him.**

When Halder was finally retired in September 1942, it was because Hitler seemed weary of their perpetual struggle. Parting would be a relief for both of them but, in ridding himself of Halder, Hitler was disposing of more than an uncooperative general.

It was not simply Halder that the Fuhrer could not get along with but everything that Halder represented. The coolness of traditional military thinking which looked at the problems of the war from an almost detached point of view was anathema to Hitler. He could not be told that certain actions would lead to defeat because he believed that willpower and morale could overcome petty details of number and supply. When Halder had gone, Hitler had been freed from the last effective tie with military reality. To be sure of this he appointed General Kurt Zeitzler, whom he reckoned to be younger and less conservative, as Halder's successor.

In fact Zeitzler did show an initial sympathy with Hitler's military ideas and he certainly never used open opposition to impose any restraints on his Fuhrer, but he did feel some kinship with the officer corps in one sphere. He tried to stand up for senior Army Officers who were more and more the subject of Hitler's criticism —even his hatred. The Fuhrer had probably always felt some rancour for the patronising patricians of the General Staff and he was well on the way to regarding any argument from a soldier as treason. He certainly made it clear that he had a preference for soldiers who were not from the charmed circle of Prussian traditionalism.

> **The role of Sepp Dietrich is unique. He is a man who is simultaneously cunning, energetic and brutal. Under his swashbuckling appearance, Dietrich is a serious conscientious, scrupulous character. He is a phenomenon in the class of people like Frundsberg, Ziethen and Seydlitz. Sepp Dietrich is a national institution.**

Sepp Dietrich, for instance, was a rough, hard-driving character who had begun as Hitler's chauffeur and bodyguard commander. His tough methods achieved a fair amount of success—which was all the more delightful to Hitler because Dietrich was not staff trained and because it was achieved through the Fuhrer's favourite virtues of energy and hardness. Dietrich was not the sort of man to question orders and that was what Hitler required.

It was, of course, a little difficult to continue ignoring professional military advice in the aftermath of Stalingrad but Hitler had a great capacity for self-delusion. To foster this and to keep reality at a distance he used a number of devices which gave him apparently legitimate cause to ignore military advice. The most deceitful of these was to claim that his soldiers could not see the whole picture: they were limited to their military function and had no idea of political implications. This hoary lie was frequently trotted out—it was even used to justify letting the British Expeditionary Force escape at Dunkirk. It cropped up during the Stalingrad disaster when Hitler convinced himself that capturing Stalingrad and Leningrad, the 'two Holy Cities of Communism', would deliver a political blow that would fell the Soviet Union. Whenever he was brought to face unpleasant military facts he could try to overrule them with more important political objectives. In this way, when the German Army had been exhausted by the battle for Kursk in 1943, he refused to accept the logic of withdrawal in the South to face the Russian winter offensive. To do so he would have to give up the Crimea and he was quick to invent a political imperative.

It was always the same: a withdrawal in the North might upset the Finns; any retreat might affect the confidence of the Rumanian or Hungarian allies. For every unpalatable military suggestion, he could produce a fine sounding reason for ignoring his generals' advice.

Even Zeitzler could not tolerate this sort of thing for ever. As time wore on, his belief in the Fuhrer's military genius became decidedly patchy. The records show that he was not the sort of man to oppose Hitler directly but that he put the case for his colleagues' point of view with increasing urgency. This temerity wedded to the steady deterioration of the military situation determined Hitler to find another Chief of Staff. In all probability he would have picked General Buhle for the post, but Buhle was badly wounded in the von Stauffenberg assassination attempt of 20 July 1944 and Hitler was forced to send for the Panzer expert, General Heinz Guderian. In the years before the war there had been an identity of interest between Hitler and the abrasive, energetic Guderian in the construction of the Panzer armoured forces. Although Guderian's later writings are impenetrable in this respect, the two men may have had a certain mutual regard for each other, Guderian's storming drive-on tactics were the sort of thing that excited Hitler's admiration. Although Guderian had been broken like so many others in the winter of 1941-42 for advocating retreat, he had since been rehabilitated as Inspector-General of Armoured Troops and Hitler no doubt hoped that he would be a positive Chief of Staff with an aggression that matched his own. In this he was to be disappointed, as the great Panzer leader had a strong streak of commonsense and a conventional staff training. In conference he was cold, correct and frequently sarcastic but, by this time, Hitler had taken such a total grip on the conduct of the war that Guderian could not hope to influence him or change his methods. After the assassination attempt which resulted in Guderian's appointment, Hitler's attitude towards the General Staff became one of open hatred.

31 AUGUST   **1944**

I accuse the General Staff of weakening combat officers who joined its ranks, instead of exuding this iron will, and of spreading pessimism when General Staff officers went to the front.

Below: *Just a few of the 13 million Germans who were to taste military life by the end of the war. Every one of them had to swear a personal oath of allegiance to the Fuhrer, supreme commander of the Armed Forces, '. . . and that as a brave soldier I will be prepared to lay down my life in pursuance of this oath at any time'.*

Once he had found that high-ranking officers in the West had intended to betray him, Hitler began to put all his failures down to the defeatism of the traditional officer corps. At the same time, the SS were busy stringing up distinguished members of that same officer corps for disloyalty so that the final humiliation of the German Army and its complete subjection to the dictator had been accomplished—even Guderian was forced to sit in a military court which had the function of handing the plotters over to the Gestapo. For his part, Hitler seemed to derive considerable satisfaction from watching the grisly executions of respected senior officers—including one aged Fieldmarshal—who were filmed in their naked death struggles as they were slowly strangled on piano wire suspended from meat-hooks.

The conventional soldiers could see by this time that Germany had lost the war. On the other hand, it is quite clear that Hitler was far from despairing. German forces were still fighting far beyond the frontiers of the Reich and the fact that they were pitted against the three most powerful nations in the world impressed him less than it did his soldiers. For a start he expected great things from the new weapons that his scientists were developing. He hoped to destroy London and other parts of Britain with V rockets launched from Holland, and believed

that this might eliminate England from the struggle. He also believed that the jets would make a great difference by reclaiming air superiority and relieving Germany from the fearful pounding of the Allied bombing offensive. He pinned a great deal of hope on the effectiveness of German technological superiority, yet even that was not as important to him as his belief in a political turn of fortune.

Not without reason, as a shrewd calculation of post-war political interests would show, he could not credit an alliance between Britain, America and Russia with durability. Again and again he compared his situation with that of Frederick the Great who was, at one stage of his spectacular career, knuckling under to an irresistable combination of European powers when, just as all seemed lost, the death of a Russian Empress caused the coalition of his opponents to dissolve. With this 'miracle' ever in front of him it was useless for soldiers to suggest that cool logic indicated that it was time to sue for peace.

27 JANUARY   1945

These things should be given to our officer corps as required reading. They have absorbed only the spirit of Schlieffen and not the spirit of Moltke, Frederick the Great, Frederick William I, Blucher, etc.

Hitler fully realized what the accepted thinking of the officer corps was, but he accused it of being too influenced by the great military thinkers of Germany's past and not showing enough of the spirit of her great captains and leaders who had often triumphed despite the odds. Things may look hopeless he claimed, but they have been just as bad in the past and still heralded a triumphant conclusion. He resented his generals' lack of faith in his destiny and was more contemptuous than ever of their rational approach.

While Hitler's 'miracle' failed to put in an appearance and the military situation became more and more desperate, the relationship between the Fuhrer and his professional soldiers became more and more antagonistic. Hitler had never been keen to face hard facts and he retreated into the beginnings of a dangerous deception. To disguise the weakness of his forces they were diluted, so that divisions were sometimes at little more than brigade strength and brigades not much more than regiments. The end of this process was found in his last days in his bunker when he directed armies and army groups which existed only in his imagination. He was deaf to all protests and criticisms and simply evasive when confronted with any bluntness. At the same time, this refusal to recognize reality resulted in ever greater cruelties to his soldiers and, especially, their officers.

An unstoppable Russian offensive in January lapped around Warsaw. Hitler had convinced himself that Warsaw was a fortress and a strongly garrisoned one. In fact there were only four battalions of fortress troops in Warsaw and, when they were ordered to break out and surrender the city rather than fight for it by realistic OKH officers, Hitler demanded blood.

18 JANUARY   **1945**

It is the General Staff I am after. It is intolerable to me that a group of intellectuals should presume to press their views on their superiors. But such is the General Staff system and that system I intend to smash.

On this occasion a number of officers were arrested but later released or captured by the advancing Allies, but it was not always so. Men were often shot upon accusations of defeatism or disobedience.

Hitler justified his hardness by claiming that he was virtually the only man among the circle of his advisers who had actually seen front line service. In fact this claim was all too true as many of the creatures with whom he was surrounded at this time had only tenuous claims to being soldiers at all. When he extolled the virtues of real combat he did so to an audience which could hardly answer back, and the corollary to stressing the virtue of the simple fighting man was to claim that those who directed him from places of safety were incompetent or, at any rate, comparatively worthless.

To the maddened, vengeful Fuhrer it seemed that the life of a General Staff officer was an absurdly easy one. Headquarters soldiering was something anyone could do and those who had trained in it were lacking in the one soldierly essential—operational experience.

In these last doomed months he had a desire to pull the whole German nation down with him. He gave orders for a scorched earth policy which would have resulted in untold suffering from an already battered nation had they not been calmly circumvented by Armaments Minister Speer who had rather higher humanitarian standards. Even the devoted *Waffen SS* could not escape censure. After their prodigious efforts to relieve Budapest had failed, they were bitterly reproached and Hitler issued his famous 'armband order' depriving them of their insignia. Everyone was reviled; everyone had failed him.

Only at the very end did Hitler's mood change when, literally within a day of his suicide, the Fuhrer became calmer. Looking back on the titanic struggle which he had unleashed, he had to admit that the German people had shown heroic courage. In his last testament he paid some sort of tribute to that, and reserved his bitterness for the friends who had betrayed him and, above all, the German General Staff. After all, someone had to take the blame for military defeat and Hitler was certainly not going to do so.

Right: *A deserter, hanged by the SS in Berlin, 1945. Few soldiers broke their oath of obedience to the Fuhrer.*

ES KANN NUR EINER
SIEGEN UND DAS
SIND WIR

GOTTFRIED
KLEIN

ADOLF HITLER AM 8. NOVEMBER 1939

Decisive battles

**France   Britain
Barbarossa   Stalingrad
Kursk   Normandy
The Ardennes   The Atlantic
Bomber offensive**

'There can only be one victor, and that is us . . .'

FRANCE

16 AUGUST   **1942**

Once conscription was introduced into Britain, the die was cast...and not in our favour. Happily they had not the patience to wait. If they had held on for three or four years, they would have had an army of 30 or 40 divisions which they could have sent to Europe.

HITLER'S TRIUMPH IN POLAND was hardly complete before he began to put pressure on his Army command to attack the Western Allies Britain and France. His motives were more than simple aggression or lust for conquest. He knew that it would be some time before the British could produce a large continental army, but that they were likely to provide increasing aid to France as the months went by. Taking that into consideration and also the eventual effects of a British blockade he was determined to strike hard and soon for, as he read the situation, his enemies grew stronger daily.

Hitler's Army High Command, however, were less enthusiastic to join battle pell mell with an enemy whom they had every cause to respect and felt that a delay would add considerably to the strength of the German Army which was by no means as large and well-equipped as it might have been in 1939.

23 NOVEMBER   **1939**

My decision is unchangeable. I shall attack France and England at the most favourable and earliest moment. Breach of the neutrality of Belgium and Holland is of no importance. No one will question that when we have won.

As it happened, the delay imposed by an unwilling Army Command was of great advantage in securing a German victory—for, in the winter months of *sitzkrieg* while nothing much happened on the Western front, the plan of attack was changed. Originally the Army High Command had been intending to use the so-called 'Schlieffen Plan' which had been so nearly successful in 1914. This involved a giant wheeling motion through Belgium and France led by the right shoulder of a mass of German armies which would have their left shoulder resting on a pivotal point about Sedan. As the German Panzer expert General Heinz Guderian remarked dryly 'this had the advantage of simplicity, though hardly the charm of novelty'. Indeed it was obvious from the disposition of the Franco-British forces that this was just what they were expecting and were prepared to move fast and fight hard to stop it.

During November 1939, one of the German Army's most gifted operational planners, General Erich von Manstein, thought of a radical alternative for the rather stale strategy of the High Command. Basically the idea was to simulate the Schlieffen plan by making a strong attack through Belgium with a heavy preponderance of Germany's infantry forces and then, as the Allies rushed to the assistance of a neutral country so unblushingly struck down, to smash through the hinge of their forward movement in the Ardennes with all the available armoured divisions, and to loop round and encircle them. The German High Command were not enamoured of Manstein's brain child because they maintained that the Panzer divisions would be held up by the French defence of the river Meuse and would have to wait for infantry to come up and force its crossing; by which time the Allies could make an appropriate response.

Manstein was demoted to command an infantry corps, but managed to put his ideas in front of Hitler who was impressed by them. Under pressure from the Fuhrer and the knowledge that the original plan had fallen into the hands of the Belgians when an aircraft carrying a courier had gone off course, the High Command agreed to change to an approximation of Manstein's plan. There were certain differences. The Panzer divisions would not be used en bloc for the single thrust through the Ardennes because the speed and cutting edge of motorized units would be needed elsewhere—especially in Holland.

26 MAY   **1939**

The Dutch and Belgian air bases must be occupied by armed force with lightning speed. Declarations of neutrality must be ignored.

Even before the outbreak of war, Hitler had determined that neutral Belgium and Holland should be occupied, because he believed that they would provide bases for an air and sea war against Britain if his armies should be held up in France. Unless Holland was taken very quickly by paratroops and highly mobile forces, large areas of its low lying countryside could be flooded which would add

Above: *The French had believed any German attack would follow the traditional invasion route—through Flanders—and the invasion of Belgium and attacks on the Maginot Line did nothing to disillusion them. Hitler claimed on 10 May 'It was wonderful . . . I could have wept for joy; they'd fallen into the trap'.*

greatly to the difficulties of attack.

The Germans had assembled 135 divisions for their attack—while the combined forces of France, Belgium, Holland and the BEF had as many as 136, but many factors gave the Germans a decisive advantage. One of them was their employment of new types of troops—paratroopers and Panzers—which were to be worth the whole of the rest of their army, although they amounted to less than ten of the divisions employed. The other advantage was that their opponents had no military alliance. The Dutch had remained neutral throughout World War I and thought that they would be able to maintain that status. On more questionable grounds the Belgians also believed that their neutrality would be respected and refused to allow the British and French to move forward for the defence of their country. Hitler was always a man ready to exploit indecision or weakness and he had continually reassured the Dutch and Belgians.

26 AUGUST   1939

Germany will in no circumstances impair the inviolability of Belgium and Holland.

The French and British were more realistic about things, and knew that the Belgians were bound to appeal to them for help once they were attacked. In order to assist Belgium, the French evolved 'Plan D' in which their Northern Army and the BEF would rush forward to meet the Germans in Belgium. The British grumbled that this would leave them at a disadvantage and sacrifice prepared positions, but agreed to conform to the fatal plan.

In the event the German plan worked like clockwork and the efforts of the French and British hastened their defeat. On 10 May airborne forces dropped on Rotterdam and the Hague while a simultaneous attack on the Dutch frontier was spearheaded by the 9th Panzer division. These novel methods of making war achieved great success, with many bridges captured intact owing to the paratroops, but the confused Dutch fought back hard.

The Belgians resisted as well as they could, but were losing the struggle as the nine divisions of the BEF and three French armies answered their appeal by advancing into the hurricane to take on the Germans along the Dyle river on the 12th. Despite the doubts of the British this forward movement was accomplished without a hitch, but none of the Allied commanders realized that they had advanced into a trap.

14 MAY   **1940**

The power of resistance of the Dutch Army has proved to be stronger than anticipated. Political as well as military considerations require that this resistance be broken speedily.

On the 14th the German hammer blows fell. Hitler had become anxious about the gallant resistance of the Dutch and ordered a resort to terror. He ordered the heavy bombing of Rotterdam. Stupefied by reports of the casualties and destruction, the Dutch capitulated that evening. By that time the Allies who had tried to aid them felt the mortal blow which the armoured column of Panzer troops had delivered behind them in the Ardennes.

When the armoured columns of the main German assault began to snake forward through the Ardennes they stretched back for 100 miles. Their spearhead was seven armoured divisions in three corps, and these were backed up by motorized infantry divisions and preceded by waves of Stuka dive-bombers. By the 14th this formidable force had brushed aside light opposition on the frontier and emerged on the banks of the Meuse—the main defensive position of the weak French forces deputed to guard the hinge of advance of their northern armies. While the Stukas kept the French gunners' heads down the Panzer engineers succeeded in bridging the Meuse, and two tank divisions poured across on the morning of the 14th to strike west. Despite frantic attempts by the Allied air forces to bomb this vital bridge it was unhit and men and materials crossed it in a seemingly unending stream. By that evening the bridgehead at Sedan was thirty miles wide and fifteen miles deep. The hinge of the Allied advance was shattered and the advance of the German motorized forces was gathering momentum.

Guderian, who commanded the XIX Armoured Corps which was in the vanguard of the Panzer thrust, was determined to motor on to Amiens and then loop up through the Channel ports to complete the encirclement of the French Northern Army group, the BEF and the 22 divisions of the Belgian Army. As a hard-driving and super-confident soldier he was sure that the faster he moved the more confused the enemy would become, and the less likely he would be to counter attack. Others were less convinced. The Panzers only provided the spearhead of the thrust and the breach they made in the Allied forces had to be kept open behind them by corridors of infantry. With the Panzers pushing on so fast, the infantry could hardly keep up and it seemed that the slim German tentacle of penetration would soon be cut off by an Allied counter-attack.

In fact the Allies had no reserves so the Germans had nothing to fear, but Hitler was uneasy. It was all going too smoothly and he had memories of the victorious German advance of August 1914 which had been turned into retreat—almost rout—by unexpected pressure on its flank. Hitler's worries were strengthened by General

Right: *When the armoured columns of the main German assault began to snake forward through the Ardennes, they stretched back for 100 miles.*

(later Fieldmarshal) Gerd von Rundstedt, the commander of Army Group A (which included the Panzer group which was delivering the main blow), who agreed that there was a danger of a French counter stroke from the south. The Fuhrer's nerve gave and, on the morning of the 17th, Guderian was given the order to halt in his tracks and hang on until the position gained had been consolidated.

18 MAY   **1940**

I am keeping an eye on this. The miracle of the Marne of 1914 will not be repeated.

While Hitler was all for playing safe, Guderian was all for going for broke. He was a third of the way to the Channel and he knew that any delay would give the shattered Allies time to regroup, realize what was happening and put some firm opposition in front of him. He put pressure on his superiors to permit him a 'reconnaissance in force' which was all the excuse he needed to set his corps rolling again.

So while Hitler spent the 17th and 18th raging at Brauchitsch, Commander in Chief of the German Army, and Halder, Chief of the German General Staff, telling them that their rashness and negligence would lose the battle, the Panzers pushed on. As the Fuhrer still concerned himself with building up forces on the southern

flank he was surprised and, to be fair, delighted to learn that the 2nd Panzer division had reached the mouth of the Somme at Abbeville on the 20th. The Allies had been cut in half, with their best troops in the north. The Fuhrer was 'beside himself with joy' and even spoke in the highest terms of the German Army and its leadership.

However, the Allies might have been cut in half but anyone with any idea of British seapower realized that they were not cut off. Before they were destroyed by encirclement it would be necessary to take the Channel ports which lay behind them—not as difficult as it ought to have been because the Allies were still heavily involved fighting in Belgium and had almost no formations which could oppose the all-conquering sweep of the Panzers. Guderian turned north from Abbeville and began to gobble up the Channel ports but, although he was able to deal with the problems caused by frantic British resistance to his progress, fears of loss and failure began to loom again in Hitler's mind.

Shattered and bewildered by the speed of the German advance, the Allies' commanders made plans which were outdated before they could be used, but the British lashed out where they could. On 21 May, as Guderian was issuing the codewords *Abmarsch Nord* for his forces to hook north, they mounted a tank attack at Arras which failed but caused panic in the SS motorized

division *Totenkopf* and badly rattled the Fuhrer. Guderian's leading Panzers found that the French garrisons and volunteers at Boulogne and Calais had been reinforced by British regiments hurriedly shipped in, and he had to fight for both ports. In Calais 3000 British troops and 800 Frenchmen were told by the French area commander that there would be no evacuation and had been exhorted by the British Foreign Secretary to 'perform an exploit worthy of the British name'. Heavily outnumbered and condemned to fight to the last, the Allies put up stout resistance which held up Guderian's advance—but not by enough to save the BEF. Although much of Guderian's corps was kept fighting in the streets of Calais, he still had plenty of troops for a push on to undefended Dunkirk— the last Channel port. Leaving 10th Panzer division and the Corps artillery to contest Calais, 1st and 2nd Panzer reached the line of the Aa canal—within sight of Dunkirk —when they were stopped by Hitler's orders on 24 May.

The Fuhrer had been a bit nervous throughout the campaign whenever resistance occurred. The Germans were not all that rich in tanks and their ten Panzer divisions had already lost a number through breakdown and occasional Allied resistance. Hitler was anxious to conserve what he had, for he did not realize that this battle for the Channel ports was decisive—he felt that he would need his armour for the conquest of the rest of

France. He also recalled from his experience of World War I that the marshy Flanders countryside was unsuitable for tanks, and the egregious Goering assured him that the Luftwaffe alone could prevent any Allied evacuation from the Channel ports. Why risk losing any more valuable AFVs in contesting Calais or Dunkirk when Goering was sure it was not necessary?

24 MAY   **1940**

Dunkirk is to be left to the Luftwaffe. Should the capture of Calais prove difficult, this port too is to be left to the Luftwaffe.

As he weighed these factors up, Hitler took the easier and, finally, unsuccessful course. He ordered Guderian to stop and although the latter's genius for insubordination

Opposite: 26 *May* 1940, *Calais falls.*
Below: *Scuttled British ships in the entrance to the Port of Dunkirk. The evacuation of the BEF was one of the most miraculous escapes since the parting of the Red Sea.*

allowed him to continue the assault on Calais which fell, after bitter fighting ,on the evening of the 26th, he was not defiant enough to push on to Dunkirk.

The fatal results of Hitler's interference are well-known although they were hardly apparent at the time. The Allies and particularly the British used their unexpected reprieve to good effect. By the evening of the 26th when Hitler's orders to stop were eventually rescinded, they had established firm defences around Dunkirk, and the Royal Navy was beginning Operation Dynamo by which a third of a million men were to be evacuated from the port and nearby beaches. Although the Belgian Army surrendered on the 28th, the Franco-British forces still managed to fend off the Germans and slip away to sea.

29 MAY   **1940**

The fate of the French Army in Artois is sealed. The British Army which has been compressed into the territory around Dunkirk is also going to its destruction before our concentric attack.

Hitler had no idea that his victory was proving incomplete and was unaware on the 29th that the Luftwaffe was not able to fulfil Goering's promise. Dunkirk itself did not fall until 4 June, and by then 338,226 French and British soldiers had got away.

Despite the halting and error caused by Hitler's interference, the Germans had won a victory so complete that the fall of France was certain. The troops who had been evacuated from Dunkirk had left without their equipment and were in no condition to contest the rest of the battle. France had lost 30 of her best divisions, the bulk of her armour and any significant assistance from the BEF, but the French still tried to contest the line of the Somme. Their struggle was hopeless, as they could deploy only 43 depleted French and two British divisions against 143 full strength German divisions, which included the formidable Panzers and enjoyed almost complete air superiority. To add to the inequality and Hitler's pleasure, Mussolini prepared to bring Italy into the war and attack France on the Alpine frontier.

Below: *Hitler, Keitel, Raeder, Goering, von Ribbentrop, von Brauchitsch and Hess in the railway carriage that had been the scene of Germany's greatest humiliation, the signing of the Versailles Treaty. The occasion, this time, was the formal French surrender, and the Reich's greatest triumph.*

If there could be anything which could strengthen my unshakable belief in the victorious outcome of this war it was the Duce's statement.

On 5 June the overwhelming German assault began and, although the outnumbered French fought with the greatest courage (inflicting double the daily loss rate which the Germans had suffered in the Dunkirk campaign), the result was a foregone conclusion. The Germans surged south in a victorious wave and, although the Italian offensive which opened on the 10th was an abject failure, the French had exhausted all possibilities of resistance when the fighting stopped on 25 June. France had fallen.

Opposite: *A traditional tourist pose, and one of Hitler's favourite pictures of his visit to Paris. He obviously felt he could afford to relax; despite the miracle of Dunkirk, the BEF had ceased to exist as a fighting unit and had lost virtually all its equipment. Britain would undoubtedly sue for peace.*

BRITAIN

HITLER WAS NOT ALONE in his belief, expressed at the beginning of July 1940, that Britain had gone down in irremediable defeat. Joseph Kennedy, America's ambassador to London, prophesied that the Fuhrer would be in London by 15 August and, throughout the world, opinion hardened that the British must be written off.

1 JULY **1940**

I cannot conceive of anyone in England still seriously believing in victory.

Simple mathematics produced the same conclusion. Even if the British were given time to rebuild the army which had been shattered in the battle for France, they could not, as a nation of some 45,000,000 people pose a credible threat to 80,000,000 Germans and their allies. Because of this manpower shortage, the British plan was to put some 50 divisions in the field by 1942, as well as maintaining the industrial production and naval power of the Western allies. These 50 divisions could have maintained the struggle alongside the 100-plus divisions of the French Army, but they could never have survived a head-on clash with the 170 divisions deployed by a fully mobilized Germany. Added to these considerations were the facts that, by July 1940, Germany was allied to Italy, supplied by Russia, and had high hopes of bringing Spain and the new French government in on the Axis side. Britain's fight seemed lonely and hopeless indeed.

Although Hitler could reasonably feel free from any fears of British retaliation, his war against Britain had not yet been brought to a suitably violent conclusion.

2 JULY **1940**

A landing in England is possible, providing that air superiority can be attained and certain other conditions fulfilled. The date of commencement is still undecided. All preparations to be begun immediately. All preparations to be undertaken on the basis that the invasion is still only a plan and has not yet been decided upon.

By 2 July Hitler was giving an uncharacteristically cautious order to prepare for an invasion of England. There was no doubt that a victory parade through London and the utter humiliation of his principal enemies had a strong appeal for the Fuhrer, but he was uneasily aware that such a project was entering unknown military territory. The truth was that the famed German General Staff had not seriously considered plans for an attack on Britain, and the planners of all three services considered it to be a perplexing problem. Because he had no clear idea as to how he would proceed to unleash a 'storm of wrath and steel' against the British, Hitler hedged his bets. He told his strategists to make their plans for a landing and even to make preparations to carry it out, but he gave no definite commitment that he would proceed with the action decided upon. He had made such vast conquests in the past few months—Denmark, Norway, Holland, Belgium and, above all, France—that he was temporarily sated. The British were in a hopeless position and their government might collapse or sue for peace. If that happened there would be no need for an invasion.

Although the British were unable to do much more than make defiant noises, they were absolutely united in their determination to fight on. Any number of neutral intermediaries found them in a mood of baffled fury and ready to reject all offers of peace in insulting terms. This unrealistic attitude began to awaken a reaction in Hitler, so that he became amazed, even affronted, by such insolence and longed to punish it.

13 JULY **1940**

I have made to Britain so many offers of agreement, even of co-operation, and have been treated so shabbily that I am now convinced that any new appeal to reason would meet with a similar rejection. In that country at present, it is not reason that rules.

Hitler had never been noted for his forbearance and his mood alternated sharply between a desire for a negotiated peace and a strong feeling that the British should be taught a savage and final lesson. As July passed, he still could not make up his mind about his course of action and, from his indecision, sprang the seeds of failure. The German generals were wary of the dangers of crossing the Channel and unlikely to carry out their preparations with enthusiasm; only the single-mindedness and determination of Hitler himself could force the invasion project forward.

Opposite: *Torquay, in the summer of* 1940.

As uncertainties crowded in on Hitler, the tentative plans of his operations staff were going ahead. From 10 July the Luftwaffe began its trial of strength with the RAF over the Channel. All the invasion plans highlighted the absolute necessity for German naval and air supremacy over the invasion routes and landing grounds if there was to be any reasonable prospect of success. In practice, the unchallengable strength of the Royal Navy meant that the invasion would have to be protected by a complete German air superiority. With morale suitably high after a string of victorious campaigns, the Luftwaffe eagerly pressed the battle against the RAF—which they judged to be of inconsiderable strength. By 16 July Hitler's patience was exhausted and he gave the fateful orders for a landing operation against England, but included the reservation that the operation should only be carried out 'if necessary'. He would make one last appeal and give the stiff-necked British one last chance.

Since England still shows no sign of willingness to come to terms, I have decided to prepare a landing operation against England and, if necessary, to carry it out.

The German Army, however, did not wait for Hitler's appeal before it executed his order. On 17 July the invasion plans were completed and 13 picked divisions were ordered to jumping-off places on the Channel coast as the first wave of assault. The Army plan for the invasion (Operation Sea Lion) was almost ludicrously

Below: *Spitfires were undoubtedly the difference between success and failure for the Luftwaffe.*

ambitious. In the first wave, six divisions were to hit the beaches between Ramsgate and Bexhill, four divisions would come ashore between Brighton and the Isle of Wight while, further west, three more divisions would land at Lyme Bay. This initial force was one of 90,000 men, to be built up to 260,000 men by the third day. There were plans for assistance from airborne forces, and for a second wave including six Panzer divisions and three motorized divisions. Within a few days it was hoped to deploy 41 complete divisions in an awesome concentration of force which the British could not hope to combat successfully.

By 19 July the German Navy had dealt a blow to the Army's grandiose schemes for conquest, by flatly announcing that it simply could not transport such vast numbers of men across the Channel on a 200 mile front in the teeth of a superior navy. On the same day, Hitler made a speech to the Reichstag in which he once again offered peace to Britain but on very unspecific terms.

In this hour I feel it to be my duty before my own conscience to appeal once more to reason and common sense in Great Britain as much as elsewhere. I consider myself in a position to make this appeal since I am not the vanquished begging favours, but the victor speaking in the name of reason. I can see no reason why this war must go on.

Below: *Free French pilots run for their Spitfires during the Battle of Britain. Although not obvious to Hitler at the time, the failure of the Luftwaffe was a key turning point in the war.*

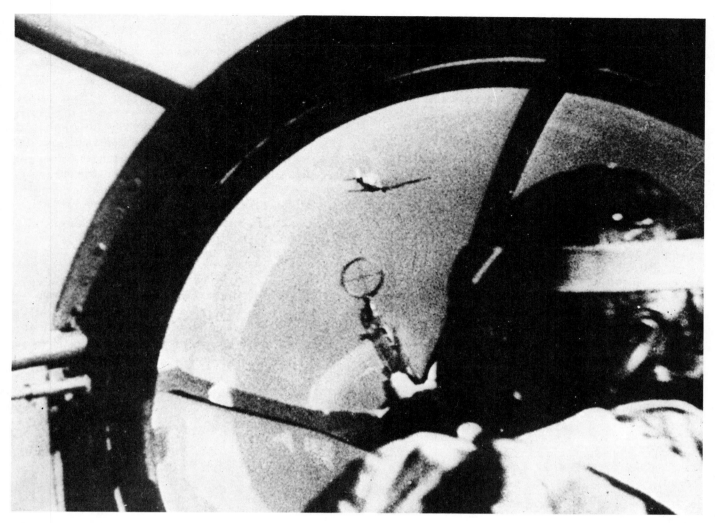

Above: *An elusive Spitfire twists away from the gun sights of a Heinkel.*

There must be some doubt whether, by this stage, the Fuhrer really wanted to let the British off so lightly, or whether his professed desire for peace was simply his usual device of presenting himself as a reasonable man to the German people and world opinion before savagely striking down an opponent. He was, it is true, slightly ambivalent towards the British, In *Mein Kampf* he had even proposed that Britain was Germany's natural ally, and he was often free with his admiration of the British achievement in the shape of their vast Empire. Yet the records show that he was not bluffing when he threatened invasion in 1940.

Secret German military files leave no doubt that the invasion project was serious and that the British were to be shown no mercy. Once the conquest had been accomplished, an even darker nightmare was to fall on the British than that which gripped tortured Poland. Nazi vengeance demanded the utter destruction of the British race, beginning with the deportation of every able-bodied male between the ages of 17 and 45. As if guessing that their fight was literally for survival, the British, on their side, were also preparing to abandon all the normal

restraints of convention. They made plans for the indiscriminate use of mustard gas and armed tens of thousands of *francs-tireurs* in the Home Guard. London was to be fought street by street, for it was better that it should be 'laid in ashes and ruins than that it should be tamely and abjectly enslaved'. The atmosphere was heavy with the threat of massacre on an unprecedented scale, as Churchill made clear on 14 July: 'We shall seek no terms. We shall tolerate no parley. We may show mercy, but we shall ask for none'.

As July progressed, it became apparent that there was one prerequisite step which the Germans had to take before they could come to grips with their enemies: the resistance of the RAF had to be smashed. The wrangles between the Army and the Navy as to whether Sea Lion should take place on a broad front or a narrow one were academic as long as powerful forces of the Royal Navy were able to operate in the Channel. When the Navy suggested that the landing should be made on a narrow front between Eastbourne and the Straits of Dover, the agitated Chief of the Army General Staff claimed that he might just as well put his troops through a sausage machine. In fact he over-estimated the strength of the British Army. Right through August the British Army could hardly deploy more than half a dozen divisions of much fighting value because so much equipment had been lost at Dunkirk. By mid-September a miracle of recovery gave it 15 useful divisions plus three armoured divisions and one armoured brigade. But it really did not matter if the British Army could not find a Corporal's Guard just so long as there was a real possibility that the Royal Navy and the RAF could sink every ship and barge the Germans might send. It was up to the Luftwaffe to give the Germans a basis for success.

However, the Luftwaffe was soon to discover that it did not have an overwhelming advantage over the RAF. It deployed three air fleets (*Luftflotten*) for the combat. Two of them operating from northern France and the Low Countries boasted 929 fighters, 875 bombers and 315 of the all-conquering Stuka dive bombers. The other air fleet was based in Scandinavia with 123 bombers and 34 twin-engined ME110 fighters. There were between 700 and 800 fighters on the British side in 53 squadrons—of which 45 were composed of the modern Hurricanes and Spitfires. So, in overall numbers, the British were not hopelessly inferior—especially since they were producing 100 new fighters a week at the height of the battle—but they had far fewer pilots than the Germans and, at one stage, these were being lost faster than they could be replaced.

During July, the Luftwaffe tried to lure the RAF into combat over the advantageous ground of the Channel by repeated attacks on British shipping. In engagements over the Channel, the Germans would be able to carry on their combat for the same length of time as the British without running short of fuel. There was also the advantage that pilots who ditched in the sea might well be rescued, while those who came down over England were lost for the duration. Despite this, the preliminary sparring showed little sign of destroying the RAF—which only committed a fraction of its fighters. In fact, the Luftwaffe lost 296 aircraft destroyed and 135 damaged during this phase of the campaign, while the RAF lost 148 fighters. The onslaught would obviously have to be stepped up—especially since Hitler was beginning to look for results.

31 JULY   **1940**

The decisive result can only be achieved by an attack on England. An attempt must therefore be made to prepare the operation for 15 September 1940. The decision as to whether the operation is to take place in September or is to be delayed until May 1941 will be made after the Air Force has made concentrated attacks on southern England for one week.

Below: *The Operations Room at Fighter Command HQ.*

On the last day of July the Fuhrer appeared to overcome his indecision to the extent of naming tentative dates for the invasion. Concentrated air attacks on southern England should soon establish whether the project could be undertaken before the rough winter seas made it impossible, or whether it would have to wait until the spring of 1941. Ominously for the future of the Reich, Hitler mused that it was only hope of Russian support that kept British hopes alive. This was nonsense, but it represented a dangerous shift in his thinking. *Mein Kampf* had made it absolutely clear that the destruction of the Soviet state was the eventual aim of the Nazi warlord, but it made sense to take on one enemy at a time. Yet Hitler's unstable temperament, with its craving for military success, was wilting under the frustration of facing an enemy who could not be reached by his beloved Panzer divisions. He was tired of his British campaign but, as an insufferable egotist, he was unwilling to back down when he had so publicly announced his intention to break the British. With demented logic he was beginning to justify a Russian campaign as a mere step in his British campaign—in this way he would not feel that he had not dared to face the challenge of the invasion.

Below: *Autumn 1940—following Hitler's fatal mistake to divert the Luftwaffe's efforts from bombing Fighter Command airfields to bombing civilian and industrial targets. This German photograph shows two Dornier 217s over London.*

The German Air Force is to overcome the British Air Force with all means at its disposal and as soon as possible.

However, there was every hope that the invasion could still go ahead as long as the RAF was destroyed first. On 1 August the Fuhrer's directive went out: the British Air Force was to be smashed in a new intensive phase of operations which was to begin on or after 6 August. The Luftwaffe responded as soon as it could and, on 12 August, provided a curtain-raiser to Operation Eagle by attacking the radar installations around England's south coast. One station was knocked out, and the horror of *Blitzkrieg* techniques came to England as bombers and screaming dive bombers pounded southern towns and ports. On the 13th and 14th, 1500 German aircraft were put in the air to attack the 11 vital fighter airfields south of London. On the 15th, Reich Marshal Goering, commander of the Luftwaffe, threw everything into the battle: 801 bombing and 1149 fighter sorties. In the south, the Germans penetrated to the suburbs of London damaging aircraft factories and airfields. As the hard-pressed RAF pilots fought to stem the raids over Kent, *Luftflotten* 5 from Scandinavia roared towards the industrial north-east which it hoped to find unprotected.

The British system of air defence, however, was conducted in depth and *Luftflotten* 5 was met by seven squadrons of Hurricanes and Spitfires, which destroyed 30 of the German planes without loss to themselves. After this disaster, *Luftflotten* 5 took no further part in the battle. In the south, the RAF was under greater pressure but it had certain advantages over its adversaries. One of these was radar information which, together with information from ground observers and the two-way link between pilots and sector stations, enabled the battle to be carefully controlled by Fighter Command. If all went well, this system meant that fighters had time to get airborn and gain height as they were directed to their enemy. Another advantage was the quality and performance of Hurricanes and the faster Spitfires. Both could be outpaced by the ME109, which also had a faster rate of climb, but the British planes were more manoeuvrable with a tighter turning circle for dogfighting, and their eight wing-mounted machine-guns soon showed that the German bombers were virtually defenceless against them.

Yet Goering's attack was making progress. On 16 August Hitler came a little closer to the vital decision as he recognized that the landing on a narrow front was the most feasible. With cold precision he made his dispositions for mass bombing of civilians, so that terror and chaos would assist his armies. Other nations had surrendered under indiscriminate bombing attacks on their capitals. Why should the British be different? As London burned they would beg for terms. The final order would not long be delayed; it only needed a clear-cut Luftwaffe victory.

Up until 19 August it looked as if the Luftwaffe was not going to deliver the victory. On 17th it lost 71 aircraft against the RAF's 27 and the carnage among the slow-moving Stuka dive bombers caused them to be withdrawn from the battle. But by the 23rd, Goering had come up with a battle-winning formula: all attacks were to be concentrated upon the fighters and fighter stations. From 24 August to 6 September the Luftwaffe sent over an average 1,000 planes a day, engaging the RAF in dogfights and bombing the airfields and vital sector stations. The RAF reeled under the assault, as five of the vital 11 forward fighter stations were heavily damaged and one had to be abandoned. During the same time, 466 British fighters were destroyed or badly damaged as against 214 German fighters and 138 bombers. In the human toll, a quarter of all available RAF pilots were killed or badly wounded.

The Germans were within an ace of victory. After a few days of this pounding, the RAF might have to abandon its forward airfields so that the Luftwaffe would have complete control over the Channel and invasion area. In the hour of crisis, Goering's successful tactics were suddenly countermanded by Hitler. The British Bomber Command had been attacking the harbours where the invasion barges assembled, but had also carried out a few token raids on Germany, including some on Berlin. This feeble retaliation for the assault on Britain provoked Hitler's fury. He promised vengeance to the German people. In response to British temerity he would have Britain's cities razed to the ground.

Below: *A devastated area of London at the height of the Blitz. However, Hitler was, unknowingly, doing Britain a favour: the Blitz granted invaluable time to Fighter Command, to train pilots, repair the airfields and build planes. Hitler's promise of vengeance almost certainly cost him the Battle.*

4 SEPTEMBER   **1940**

When the British Air Force drops two or three or four thousand kilograms of bombs then we will, in one night, drop 150-, 230-, 300- or 400,000 kilograms. When they declare that they will increase their attacks on our cities, then we will raze their cities to the ground.

Obediently the tactics were changed. On the afternoon of 7 September, 625 bombers and 648 fighters were despatched to London. The city was already blazing by nightfall, but the bombers kept coming through the night and returned the next evening. On 15 September the Luftwaffe made a huge daylight raid of 200 bombers escorted by 600 fighters but, by this time, the RAF had

had a week to recover from the blows dealt against their airfields. In a great air battle, 56 German planes were destroyed and many more had to be ditched through lack of petrol on the return. Fighter Command lost only 26 aircraft. The scales had turned at last. Hitler's desire to be revenged by bombing British cities cost him the battle.

On 14 September, Hitler was still optimistic that the Luftwaffe was winning. A landing was still the best way to finish the British off, if only the RAF could be destroyed. The great air battle of the 15th put paid to these illusions

14 SEPTEMBER   **1940**

A successful landing followed by an occupation would end the war in a short time. England would starve. A landing need not necessarily be carried out within a specified time, but a long war is not desirable. Four or five days of decent weather would bring the decisive results, but the enemy recovers again and again. Enemy fighters have not yet been completely eliminated. Our own reports of success do not give a completely reliable picture, although the enemy has been severely damaged. In spite of all our successes the prerequisite conditions for Operation Sea Lion have not yet been realized. The operation will not be renounced yet. Bombing with the object of causing a mass panic must be left to the last.

and, by the 17th, the German Navy staff noted that Operation Sea Lion was to be postponed indefinitely. Goering managed to drag the battle on into October but, by then, it was becoming too late for an invasion and the RAF was still in business. On 12 October, Hitler recognized the inevitable, for the first time the German war machine had met with a reverse.

12 OCTOBER   **1940**

I have decided that from now on until the spring, preparations for Sea Lion shall be continued solely for the purpose of maintaining political and military pressure on England. Should the invasion be reconsidered in the spring or early summer of 1941, orders for a renewal of operational readiness will be issued later.

BARBAROSSA

When we speak of new territory in Europe, we must think principally of Russia and her border vassal states. This colossal empire in the East is ripe for dissolution.

HITLER'S DETERMINATION TO DESTROY RUSSIA was part of the earliest expression of his political philosophy, and was probably hardened by his opinion that the Slavs were an inferior race created for Aryan exploitation, and by his dislike of Communism. Hitler also felt that the enterprise needed no more justification than that Germany needed the *lebensraum* or living space of the vast areas in the East.

However faithfully the Russians adhered to the provisions of the Pact that they had agreed with Hitler before the outbreak of war, their doom was sealed as a fundamental part of Nazi philosophy.

18 OCTOBER   **1939**

Occupied Poland is to be used as an assembly area for future German operations.

The fact that Hitler's mind was turning to an assault on the Eastern colossus should have become apparent to his generals a long while before he actually told them of his intentions. From the fall of Poland, the Chief of the General Staff, General Franz Halder, noted uneasily that he had not finished his business there. He announced that future German military operations would be launched from occupied Poland. Any alarm which his soldiers felt at this earlier cryptic information should have been fanned by the Fuhrer's frantic urgency to launch a knockout blow in the West. He needed the Western powers out of the way so that he could have a free hand in the East.

23 NOVEMBER   **1939**

We can oppose Russia only when we are free in the West.

Hitler never felt happy about his pact with Stalin.

Apart from his ideological distaste for it, he was frightened by Russian military ambitions. He had nightmares that the Russians would take advantage of his involvement in the West and he referred to Stalin as a 'cold-blooded blackmailer'. It was a generally accepted tenet of military wisdom that Germany should avoid a war on two fronts, and it had been concluded that the alliance between Russia and France might well have cost her World War I. Hitler was such a keen student of military history that he was well aware of the disadvantages of a two-front war. But, once he was freed of restraint in the West it should have been obvious which way his armies would be turned next.

Since the war, some of his generals have claimed that Hitler violated the sacred principle of avoiding a two-front war as he invaded Russia before he had conquered Britain, but this is hardly correct. The war between Britain and Germany was confined to side shows for some years and, if Germany was obliged to keep large garrisons in France and Norway, the troops of these garrisons were not exhausted in battle or in need of equipment replacements.

If the British found it hard to come at the Germans, there were similar difficulties for the Germans to reach

them. After the fall of France, Hitler found the whole war in the West a frustrating and profitless exercise as the RAF and the Royal Navy blocked his way. His Navy chiefs urged him to strike at the British position in the Mediterranean, but the Fuhrer was unconvinced by their plans and politically inhibited because the Mediterranean was the agreed preserve of his ally Mussolini. As so often with Hitler, he reached the conclusions he wanted to by specious reasoning.

31 JULY   **1940**

If Russia is smashed, Britain's last hope will be shattered. Then Germany will be master of Europe and the Balkans. In view of these considerations Russia must be liquidated.

By a fairly tortuous argument Hitler professed that an attack on Russia was virtually an attack on England because it destroyed British hopes of a Russian alliance. Even before he called off his invasion of Britain he was considering a Russian campaign.

By the close of the momentous year 1940, Hitler was giving instructions to his generals to prepare a Russian invasion which was later to be code-named *Barbarossa*. In their accounts of the war, almost all German generals have claimed that they were horror-struck by these proposals, and remembered the awful fate of the Swedish King Charles XII and Napoleon when these two military conquerors tried their hands at attacking Moscow.

18 DECEMBER   **1940**

The German Armed Forces must be prepared to crush Soviet Russia in a quick campaign before the end of the war against England. Preparations are to be completed by 15 May 1941. The mass of the Russian Army in western Russia is to be destroyed in daring operations by driving forward armoured deep wedges, and the retreat of intact, battle-ready troops into the wide spaces of Russia is to be prevented. The ultimate objective of the operation is to establish a defence line running from the Volga River to Archangel.

Opposite: *June 1941, Germany invites a war on two fronts with the invasion of Russia.*

In effect, as the content of Hitler's directive makes clear, there was nothing in it to remind anyone of these unsuccessful advances deep into Russia—particularly as memories of Germany's shattering defeat of Russia in World War I were still green. It is unlikely that the German commanders concerned themselves much with the ghosts of Napoleon's Grand Army as they busied themselves with plans to bring about another Treaty of Brest-Litovsk. Admittedly the Fuhrer wanted to go further than Brest-Litovsk, which had simply removed from Russia a vast area of her western provinces, 32 per cent of her population, one third of her railway mileage, 73 per cent of her iron, 89 per cent of her coal, 5000 factories and obliged her to pay an indemnity; but Germany had defeated Russia in World War I with her right arm tied behind her back on the Western front. With all available forces, the German High Command did not despair of a total and smashing victory.

There were similarities between the German plans for 1914-18 and 1941. On the former occasion Russian armies had obligingly come stumbling out of Russia to attack Germany, but had been comprehensively and repeatedly beaten by inferior German forces. The Germans had sensibly come to the conclusion that the Russians could best be beaten in Europe, and their plans provided for the Panzers to penetrate and encircle the Russian armies and to prevent the retreat of intact formations into the wide spaces of Russia. This was their rather vague objective at the beginning of the campaign—Moscow was not mentioned—and when it was accomplished they would push on into Asia to form a defensive line far east of Leningrad, Moscow and Stalingrad. As Hitler approved these mighty objectives, he was ecstatic—the World would hold its breath.

3 FEBRUARY   **1941**

When Barbarossa commences, the World will hold its breath and make no comment.

There is no doubt that the Fuhrer's megalomania, never much concealed, had been fatally aroused by his rapid conquests of Poland, Denmark, Norway, Holland, Belgium and France. The sheer scale of the operations now planned were enough to excite him. Against the 150 Russian divisions in the west, the Germans would mount a three-pronged attack by 136 divisions backed by nine line-of-communications divisions. The Germans hoped to make up for the disparity in strength by superior equipment and technique. For, although 54 of the Russian divisions were described as tank or motorized divisions, they were far from mobile—they simply did not have the motorized transport to keep all the divisional elements rolling along with the tanks. By 1941 the Germans had 21 Panzer divisions, and despite the fact that they represented only 3,550 tanks compared with 24,000 Russian tanks (of which at least half were in the west) the sheer pace at which they could move was enough to outmanoeuvre the Russians.

The Germans were assembled for the attack in three Army Groups. The centre of gravity was in the powerful Army Group Centre which, together with Army Group North, would attack north of the natural barrier of the Pripet marshes. The vast spaces of southern Russia were to be left to Army Group South. The Panzer divisions were divided into four Panzer Groups (later Panzer Armies) each of four or five Panzer divisions and three motorized divisions. Army Group Centre had two Panzer Groups to provide its cutting edge and the other Army Groups had one each. Once these titanic dispositions had been made there was an unlooked for and fatal interruption of plan.

27 MARCH 1941

The beginning of the Barbarossa operation will have to be postponed for up to four weeks.

In an excess of rage at an anti-German political coup in Yugoslavia carried out on 25 March, Hitler sent some of his forces pouring south to mop up the Balkans. The blow fell on 6 April, and Yugoslavia was struck down within a week; within three weeks Greece was also over-run and another British Expeditionary Force was turned out of Europe with a severe hiding. The German movement had been quick, but a little bit of the vital summer was gone and the Russian winter was a fraction nearer before *Barbarossa* began.

At the beginning of May Hitler had formulated his ideas on the planned course of operations against Russia. He turned down suggestions from his Panzer generals that they should push really deep into Russia—as far as the River Dnieper in Army Group Centre's case—before pinching in to encircle the Russians. That was far too risky and Hitler agreed with his more conservative generals at OKW—the Army High Command—that his enemies could be destroyed in far shallower battles of encirclement near the frontier. This divergence from the recommendations of the tank tactics experts was not to be without importance but, on the eve of the assault, Hitler expressed nothing but calm and relief that his relationship with Russia was over.

As the great offensive rolled forward it met with vast and immediate success because the Russians were taken completely by surprise. Their aircraft were destroyed on the airfields, bridges were captured intact and some artillery did not respond to the German barrage. One interested German Army officer heard a Russian radio question 'We are being fired on. What shall we do?' which

received the infuriated reply 'You must be insane and why is your signal not in code?' Within a few days the armoured pincers were closing in behind front line Russian units. The first encirclement on the central front reached back 100 miles through Slonim, but remnants of two Russian armies were able to escape it. Another 100 miles back the Panzers closed a steel ring around the Russians, who still fought desperately, at Minsk. Over 300,000 prisoners and huge quantities of material were taken in these two great sweeps into Russia, but they had not cut deep enough: many Russians escaped before the pincers closed and they still had fresh troops behind them. To destroy these forces Hitler's armies would have to go beyond the Dnieper.

5 JULY 1941

To those who ask me whether it will be enough to reach the Urals as a frontier, I reply that for the present it is enough for the frontier to be drawn back as far as that. In case of necessity we shall renew our advance wherever a new centre of resistance is formed. Moscow must disappear from the Earth's surface.

The Minsk trap had been closed on 2 July, stirring Hitler's megalomania to new heights, and, as soon as the infantry had come up, the Panzers raced forward again to thrust beyond the Dnieper in two convergent arms which were to meet at Smolensk—trapping another 300,000 Russians. Even this was not deep enough, however, and considerable Russian forces had fought their way out of the bag. Moscow was 200 miles on, and the weary Germans prepared for yet another bite at their foe. There was, however, both literally and figuratively, grit in the German war machine. A lot of the advance had been conducted over the tracks which passed for Russian roads and, when they were dry, their dust clogged the tank engines; when they were doused by a sudden shower, they turned to mud and bogged down the wheeled transport.

But it was not fatigue that stopped the advance on Moscow from the second week of August—when the battles around Smolensk were as good as over—until 2 October: that was the fault of another of Hitler's disastrous interventions in the conduct of operations. While his generals wanted to push on to Moscow he wanted to switch one of Army Group Centre's all important Panzer Groups to help Army Group North beleaguer Leningrad, and he wanted the other to turn south to help Army Group South in another vast encircling movement. The generals pointed out that Moscow was a great communications and industrial centre as well as a political objective—its capture could end the war.

Above: *Street defences in Moscow.*

21 AUGUST 1941

I am not in agreement with the proposals submitted by the Army for the prosecution of the war in the East and dated 18 August. Of primary importance before the onset of winter is not the capture of Moscow but rather the occupation of the Crimea, of the industrial and coalmining areas of the Donetz basin, the cutting of the Russian supply routes from the Caucasian oilfields and, in the North, the investment of Leningrad and the establishment of contact with the Finns.

The wrangle continued, but Hitler gave no ground. Army Group Centre must mark time while its Panzers went north and south. When the Panzer General Heinz Guderian flew to Hitler's headquarters to beg him to reconsider a decision which would send Guderian's Panzer Group on a 600 mile round trip, which men and machines could hardly stand, he was rebuffed. Whenever Hitler felt that he could not win a military argument with his generals, he resorted to giving them specious political or economic justifications for insisting on having his own way. He told Guderian that the campaign in southern Russia was dictated by economic imperatives.

23 AUGUST 1941

The Crimea is a Soviet aircraft carrier for attacking the Rumanian oilfields. My generals know nothing of the economic aspects of making war.

Obedient to orders, Guderian raced south to meet the Panzer Group of General Ewald von Kleist which was looping round the 1,000,000 strong Army Group which Russian Marshal Semyon Mikhailovich Budenny was using to defend Kiev and the Ukraine. Army Group South had already enjoyed conspicuous success and taken over 100,000 prisoners, but the new co-operation with Guderian's forces brought about one of the most spectacular victories in history. Hitler was never sated with victory. Long before Guderian and Kleist had completed the encirclement of Budenny's troops by joining hands at Lokhvista, 125 miles east of Kiev, he was urging Central Army Group on again—although he had denuded it of mobile troops.

5 SEPTEMBER 1941

The central front must get started within eight to ten days. Encircle them, beat them, destroy them.

Above: *Graphic posters were used to boost
the astonishing resistance of the Russian forces.
This one appeared in the streets of Stalingrad.*
Opposite: *Not all Russians were loyal to
Stalin. Makeshift units were recruited from
many of the conquered territories—although
Hitler had little regard for them, and in some
cases was in total ignorance of their existence.*

The operation now in progress, an encirclement with a radius of more than 1000 kilometres, has been regarded by many as impracticable. I had to throw all my authority into the scales to force it through.

By 16 September the ring around the Russian defenders of Kiev was complete and their destruction assured. When he heard the news Hitler was exultant. He knew he had scored a massive tactical success and he crowed that this was one victory which was absolutely down to him— he had had to 'throw all my authority into the scales to force it through'. It was undoubtedly a great success and the Germans took 600,000 prisoners while the dead and the booty of the battlefield, from tanks to trucks and guns, were uncounted. Yet in that spectacular success lay the seeds of failure—by the time Guderian's Panzer Group was sent north again to get Army Group Centre on the move, they might have taken Moscow not Kiev.

A capitulation of Leningrad is not to be accepted even if offered. I have decided to have Leningrad wiped off the face of the earth. The intention is to close in on the city and raze it to the ground by artillery and continuous air attack. Requests that the city be taken over will be turned down, for the problem of the survival of the population and of supplying it with food is one which cannot and should not be solved by us.

As far as Hitler was concerned Moscow was already taken—and Leningrad too if it came to that—for he was drunk with success. All restraint was set aside as he envisaged acts of world-shaking ferocity: Leningrad was to be wiped off the face of the earth. He now believed himself to be the greatest conqueror in history and he re-

Below: *A Cossack's unit, loyal to Stalin, grouping for an attack.*

flected on the sort of figure that he would cut to future generations. They were an unimaginative lot, future generations, he thought; they could never appreciate the strain he had been through to achieve his perfect military operations.

3 OCTOBER   **1941**

I declare today, and I declare it without any reservation that the enemy in the East has been struck down and will never rise again.

One thing the Fuhrer was sure of as his Panzers set off once more storming along the road to Moscow—it was all over bar the shouting. The Russian had been laid in the dust and could never rise again. By 15 October Army Group Centre had reached Mozhaisk, just 65 miles from Moscow, and it had put another 600,000 prisoners in the bag. Even then, if Hitler had used all four of the disparate Panzer Groups for a concentrated thrust on the capital it might have been his, but he was so convinced that Russia was finished that he was greedy—he kept them driving for Leningrad and the Caucasus as well as Moscow, and he was slow to feel the alarm of approaching winter and failure.

28 OCTOBER   **1941**

Fast moving units should seize the Oka bridges to the east of Serpuchov.

Even towards the end of October, Hitler was urging his 'fast moving units' on, completely blind to the fact that they hardly existed any more. Breakdowns and casualties had turned them into skeleton forces which strong Russian resistance was tying down in front of Moscow. Slowly the reality of the situation dawned on the Fuhrer—after close on 4,000,000 casualties Russia was still in business. He became despondent about his ability ever to destroy the Soviet colossus and, in a rare moment of humility early in November, he began to talk of something less than total victory.

9 NOVEMBER   **1941**

The recognition that neither force is capable of annihilating the other will lead to a compromise peace.

However, if Hitler was wavering, his generals at OKH still had their sights firmly fixed on Moscow. They wanted victory just as badly as their Fuhrer—especially since they had their Army strung out in the depths of Russia with winter approaching. They had to deliver the blow that would end the campaign, or share the fate of Napoleon's Grand Army.

15 NOVEMBER   **1941**

One final heave and we shall triumph.

Desperately, Brauchitsch, Commander in Chief of the German Army, urged Hitler to push on. On 12 November Halder reported that Russian resistance was on the verge of collapse and Hitler was convinced. But the Russian climate was about to bring its doughty assistance to the hard-pressed Soviet forces. On 3 November the thermometer began to drop deep below freezing and on the 7th the first severe cases of frostbite were reported in the German Army. By the 13th, guns and machines were failing to function in 40° of frost, and by the 21st Guderian was claiming that his forces had reached the end and could do no more.

The General Staff and the Fuhrer were determined that the attack should go on and, on 1 December, the remains of three Panzer groups were forced to struggle on against heroic Russian resistance. On 3 December a reconnaissance battalion was driven out of a Moscow suburb and by the 5th the Germans had been held everywhere in temperatures approaching 70° of frost. Just as the German generals were contemplating withdrawal for their miserable troops, who had not even been given a full issue of winter clothing, the Russians dealt them a hammer blow. General Georgi Zhukov fell on them with 100 divisions that they had not known existed. The shock broke Brauchitsch's nerve and with the Russians lapping around their strung-out units it seemed as though the German Army might well be utterly destroyed.

20 DECEMBER   **1941**

The troops must dig in where they are and hold every square yard of ground. I believe that I am entitled to ask any German soldier to lay down his life.

2 JANUARY   **1942**

The front will remain where it is regardless of consequences.

Amid the consternation and the panicky withdrawals, Hitler's granite determination and cruel indifference to his soldiers' suffering saved complete rout. There was no military science behind his orders, just a bleak unwillingness to accept any pullback. Generals were cashiered in droves as they made inevitable retreats. It was a crude and brutal strategy but it achieved its ends. Only unreason could have stabilized the German front in that terrible winter and that was something the Fuhrer had plenty of. Yet willpower alone could not stop the Russians and, by the end of February, the Germans had been pushed from 75 to 200 miles back from Moscow. The whole adventure had cost them over 1,000,000 casualties of which 250,000 were in the killed or missing bracket. That was a terrible blow to the invincible German Army and, although the Russians had taken the greater punishment losing 4,000,000 men, the vast reserves of the Soviets could better make good such heavy losses—4,000,000 Russian reservists were mobilized in 1941 alone. The Germans were to gain many more victories in Russia, but the failure in front of Moscow meant that Hitler could not deliver the quick knockout blow that he had planned.

Below: *A fate met by millions on the Russian front. This German froze to death, a victim of Hitler's determination to avoid a rout after the defeat in front of Moscow. Indeed, Generals were cashiered as they ordered inevitable retreats.*

STALINGRAD

STALINGRAD WAS THE WORST DISASTER ever suffered by the German Army and it was all of Hitler's own making. The ideas behind the campaign were born towards the end of the long and harrowing winter of 1941-42 during which the Wehrmacht had had its first taste of failure. Through this difficult time, the Fuhrer had suffered from the strain he had imposed on himself by taking over as Commander in Chief of the German Army at the height of the danger in December 1941. For two nerve-wracking months he nurtured hopes of initiating a decisive change of fortune on the Eastern Front by going over to a titanic offensive in the summer of 1942—when his soldiers would be able to put the difficulties of the Russian winter behind them. Before the end of February he was plotting the vengeance that would fall on the Russians, and expressing his delight that the months of taking punishment rather than dishing it out were over.

27 FEBRUARY   **1942**

Now that January and February are past, our enemies can give up the hope of our suffering the fate of Napoleon. They have lost nothing by waiting. Now we are about to switch over to squaring the account. What a relief.

To make sure that this final blow against the Russians had the maximum force behind it, Hitler sent his henchmen scouring through the capital cities of his allies and satellites to ask for troops. By the time he was ready to launch his summer campaign, he commanded 217 divisions and 20 brigades of which 178 divisions, eight brigades and four air forces were German. This meant that Rumanian, Hungarian and Italian allies were providing 20 per cent of the numerical strength of the Nazi armies. With a contingent of 800,000 troops from the Reich's allies, the Wehrmacht totalled 6,000,000 men armed with 3,250 tanks and self-propelled guns, 55,000 guns and mortars and assisted by an Eastern Luftwaffe with 3,500 planes. The Russians probably started the summer with a slight numerical inferiority but were rapidly making good their losses from a vast pool of millions of reservists, and a mass production tank programme which was several times greater than the Axis equivalent.

Hitler could still count on a substantial technical superiority in the techniques of contemporary warfare. The only problem that occurred to him in early 1942 was to pick the spot at which the Russians were to take the

annihilating blow he planned to deliver. In the north his besieging armies looked certain to strangle the final resistance of the heroic garrison and population of Leningrad; in the centre it seemed obvious that the Russians were expecting him to make another push for Moscow; but, in the wide spaces of south Russia, the Wehrmacht's ability to outmanoeuvre the Soviet armies could surely be used to good effect. The alternative argument—which his senior military advisers failed to put—was that the immense distance and tenuous communications of the south Russian steppes would stretch even his great army, while a concentration of force in the north to take Leningrad would assure the Wehrmacht of a secure flank along the Baltic. The Fuhrer was not that impressed by military arguments anyway, and tended to trump them by claiming that a higher necessity—economic or political—dictated his chosen course.

1 JUNE   **1942**

If I do not get the oil of Maikop and Grozny then I must end this war.

In 1942, Hitler had fixed his greedy gaze on the oil of the Caucasus and used his traditional argument of economic necessity to convince his generals of the need for a southern campaign. In fact Hitler showed himself well able to carry on the war for years without Caucasian oil, but there was a beguiling rationality behind his arguments. The Axis oil supply was tight—the Maikop and Grozny wells would ease it. A German occupation of the Caucasus could hopefully cut off the Soviet Army's oil supply and finish off its combat capacity. Most tempting of all was the area's geography: if the Caucasus could be taken, there were ready made defences to help the Nazis hold it. The Don and Volga rivers were both major military obstacles which could protect the northern flank of a Caucasian colony. There was of course the narrow isthmus that stretched between the two rivers, dominated by the great industrial city and communications centre of Stalingrad—but holding Stalingrad and the defensive lines of the rivers should be child's play now that the Russian Army was so weakened. It was all a dream: the rivers froze solid in winter and could be crossed by the heaviest armour, and the Russian Army was growing stronger, not weaker, all the time.

Things still looked promising to the Fuhrer in June 1942. His moves on the Caucasus and Stalingrad had been preceded by a Russian offensive towards Kharkov which had been emphatically defeated. The Wehrmacht destroyed three Russian armies totalling 300,000 men before setting off fast and furiously to the Caucasus. Elsewhere, the Japanese were over-running the Far East and the British Eighth Army had been forced into headlong retreat towards the Egyptian border. The Axis looked set for victory on all fronts.

Even as the Panzers sliced through the Russian opposition between the Don and Donetz rivers with their customary dash, Germany's infantry divisions were busy settling old scores in the Crimea. They had a hard, slogging fight to prize the Russian garrison out of Sebastopol, but managed it by the beginning of July—allowing the southern flank of the German onrush to rest tidily on the Black Sea while the infantrymen set off on the heels of the Panzer spearheads.

1 JULY   1942

Let us rejoice over the fall of Sebastopol.

The German Army however, should have been wary of success, for every triumph went to Hitler's head and led him to demand more of his soldiers—more than they could deliver.

On 23 July Hitler decided that his armies would have enough strength to take Stalingrad and the Caucasus at the same time. When he was given a report that the Russians could muster up to 1,250,000 fresh troops in the region north of Stalingrad and west of the Volga, that they had 500,000 men in the Caucasus and were producing 1200 front-line tanks a month, he 'flew at the man who was reading with clenched fists and foam in the corners of his mouth and forbade him to read any more'. Hundreds of thousands of German troops were then sent to a miserable death, although spectacular successes were gained in the short run.

5 AUGUST   1942

In the East it will be all over once we have cut their communications to the South and to Murmansk. Without oil they are finished.

At the beginning of August everything looked possible and the Wehrmacht was still going forward. In reality the Russian dictator Stalin had become aware of the direction of the German thrust by mid-July, and was pumping just enough by way of men and materials into Stalingrad to make sure it could put up an epic defence. By early August he had 190,000 men, 350 tanks, 340 planes and 8,000 guns or mortars on the Stalingrad front.

Below: *War-weary German troops on the outskirts of Stalingrad.*

Admittedly the German forces deputed to press on to Stalingrad had a heavy numerical superiority with 250,000 men, 750 tanks, 1200 planes and 7,500 guns or mortars, but the Russians were ready for them.

By the end of August, the German advance was slowing up but seemed to be within an ace of its final objectives. On 21 August the Swastika was hoisted on Mount Elbrus; on the 23 August General Friedrich Paulus's Sixth Army smashed through to the Volga north of Stalingrad; two weeks later the Fourth Panzer Army was set to drive through the city's southern suburbs to the great river. As it looked increasingly likely that the Russian defenders would be hemmed in with their backs to the Volga, Stalin sent for the ruthless, effective Marshal Georgi Konstantinovich Zhukov and made him Deputy Supreme Commander-in-Chief. Zhukov was as careless with Russian lives as Stalin, and he pepped up Russian resistance by frequent recourse to the firing squad for those who failed him.

28 AUGUST 1942

As regards the Russians, their powers of resistance are inimitable—as they proved in the Russo-Japanese War. This is no new characteristic they have suddenly developed.

Hitler was still confident on 28 August, but even he was beginning to take note of the Russian resistance. He convinced himself, however, that the worst was over and urged his stretched armies on to what he hoped would be the final lap. The men in the Caucasus were to take the Grozny oilfields and round off that push on the shores of the Caspian Sea. The armies around Stalingrad were to snuff out resistance there and then, as if that was not enough, prepare for a drive northwards to take Moscow from the east.

2 SEPTEMBER 1942

For as long as the war lasts, Churchill will remain. But I do not regard it as beyond the realms of possibility that some event like, perhaps, the fall of Stalingrad, may compel him to make a complete *volte face.*

The taking of Stalingrad itself began to assume more and more importance to Hitler. It was almost as though he believed that the fall of that one city would be enough to determine the war. With his attention riveted so

Below: *The Sixth Army surrenders, and the Battle of Stalingrad is lost.*

Hitler believed the capture of Stalingrad would compensate for the defeat before Moscow in the disastrous winter of 1941-42. But the German war machine was over-stretched yet again, and the winter of 1942-43 was just as bad.

closely on the objective, Hitler forgot or ignored the fact that the German armies which provided the spearhead of the attack had left long, thinly protected flanks behind them in their onrush. The left flank lay along the Don River, but it was not in a tidy position for defence. Paulus's armies had moved so quickly that they had no chance of mopping up all the Russian pockets on their way. This meant that the Soviets had retained a number of bridgeheads on the right bank of the Don—including an important foothold far to the German Sixth Army's rear, west of Serafimovitch. Added to the difficulties of a basically weak flank were those of the quality and quantity of troops defending it. Along the 350 mile length of the Don flank—from Stalingrad to Veronezh—were three satellite armies: the Hungarian Second, the Italian Eighth and the Rumanian Third. On the right flank of the Stalingrad position, which should have extended along the Volga but ran instead through the naked steppes, was the Rumanian Fourth Army. These allied troops were not only less committed than the Germans but less well equipped—they just did not possess the mobility and fire-power to defend huge sectors from determined Soviet attack.

6 SEPTEMBER   1942

The concentration of effort in the defence of Stalingrad is a grave mistake on the part of the Russians. The victor in war is he who commits the fewest number of mistakes and has also a blind faith in victory. It does prove that a name can give to a place an importance which bears no relation to its intrinsic value. For the Bolsheviks it would have been an evil omen to lose Stalingrad—and so they still hold Leningrad.

Rarely can Hitler have made a misjudgement as severe as that of 6 September. The Russians were far from concentrating their efforts in the defence of Stalingrad and were, in fact, building up their strength along the tenuous flanks of the German spearhead. As for the names of Stalin and Lenin holding such mystic significance to Communists that they would be deluded into putting all their forces into the defence of Stalingrad and Leningrad, it seems more probable that Hitler was the one who had his priorities wrong. It was he who insisted against reason that his troops take Stalingrad even when the cost of such an objective was becoming higher and higher.

The city itself was the scene of the bitterest fighting of the war. Smashed to rubble by the non-stop raids of the Luftwaffe, its ruined buildings were contested street by street. The population joined the defending troops in savaging the Germans every step of the way. 'Comrade,

Above: *The ruins of Stalingrad produced some of the most bitter street fighting of the war.*

kill your German' became the universal catchphrase as Russian guerillas joined their infantry in sniping or raiding German dugouts after dark. This was the grinding down stage of the battle, planned by Zhukov to wear his enemy out before he delivered the killer blow. Until the Volga froze over in November, the astonishing resistance of the Russian defenders of Stalingrad was nourished only by the thin trickle of supplies and reinforcements that could be smuggled across the river in small boats. What it cost them in courage and casualties is beyond computation, but it was tearing the heart out of the Germans—who lost 750,000 men, 900 tanks, 1,800 guns and 1,500 planes in the summer and autumn of the Stalingrad struggle.

The slow progress of his Army might have annoyed Hitler, but he was not unduly impressed by evidence of the strength of the Russian resistance. After all, he reckoned to know all about the hard slog of battles of attrition from his personal experience of Flanders in World War I. Besides, as he never tired of pointing out, he could be at least as stubborn as his opponents.

8 NOVEMBER   **1942**

In me they have found an adversary who does not think of the word 'capitulation'.

To the Fuhrer it was impossible to break off the struggle before he had attained the victory he had set his heart on. While he blindly urged the men of Sixth Army forward, Zhukov had assembled 1,000,000 men on the flanks of the Stalingrad salient in two groups of six armies.

On 19 November the Russians began their counter-attack, its weight falling chiefly on the Rumanian Third and Fourth Armies which stood guard on either side of Paulus's spearhead. Within four days, the Russians had cut through the flanks and were attacking Sixth Army and Fourth Panzer Army in the rear. In the course of delivering this decisive blow they had taken 250,000 Axis soldiers prisoner. The time had come for the Germans to cut their losses and try to fight their way out of the encirclement while they had a chance. The trouble was that Hitler's immediate reaction to the Russian offensive showed that he was not experiencing any sudden rush of sanity. After all the blood and effort spent in reaching the Volga he was not giving it up—whatever the cost.

20 NOVEMBER   **1942**

I will not leave the Volga. I will not go back from the Volga.

The Fuhrer ordered Sixth Army to hold fast and sent for the brilliant Fieldmarshal Erich von Manstein to organize a relief column for the encircled Paulus. On 12 December Manstein set his Panzer columns rolling, but his hopes were not high. Sixth Army was well trapped and Manstein himself was far from a secure base—as were the German troops in the Caucasus, who seemed to be even further into the noose than he was. The situation looked likely to become even more messy and it was not helped by German mistrust of the staying power of their allied troops. This was a doubt that Hitler shared. He was always keen to load the blame for failure onto someone else and he was quick to make out that he had been let down by unreliable troops. By 21 December Manstein's soldiers were within 30 miles of Stalingrad, but their own flanks were threatened far behind them on the Don where the

Italian Eighth Army had been smashed. By a miracle of soldiering, Manstein forced his way back and held the neck of the bag open long enough for the German armies in the Caucasus to escape; but he had to abandon Paulus's Sixth Army and Fourth Panzer Army.

When the troops in Stalingrad had first been encircled, Hitler had ordered the Luftwaffe to keep them supplied with food and ammunition. Bad weather and heavy losses made this an impossible undertaking, and Paulus's troops were freezing and starving to death. On 24 January the Russians offered Paulus the chance of surrender. It was not the first time, and Hitler rejected it out of hand.

24 JANUARY   **1943**

Surrender is forbidden. Sixth Army will hold their positions to the last man and the last round and by their heroic endurance will make an unforgettable contribution toward the establishment of a defensive front and the salvation of the Western World.

From his headquarters in Rastenburg, East Prussia, Hitler sent Paulus ringing messages full of National Socialist ardour and forbidding any capitulation. Sixth Army must hold on until spring when he would have another push for Stalingrad.

Inside the trap it was obvious that resistance, however heroically maintained, was not going to last until spring. The Russians had whittled the Germans down into two pockets and they simply did not have the fuel and food to maintain life—let alone a fight. Gradually this dawned on Hitler, and his belief in the survival of his grip on the banks of the Volga was replaced with a new obsession: Sixth Army must fight to the last man as an example of courage and endurance. On 30 January he made Paulus a Fieldmarshal as a final treat to reconcile him to a heroic end.

30 JANUARY   **1943**

There is no record in military history of a German Fieldmarshal being taken prisoner.

As a gesture it was a failure because Paulus surrendered the next day with 25 other generals and the remnants of his armies. Since the beginning of Zhukov's counter-attack, 32 Axis divisions and three brigades had been completely destroyed, and another 16 divisions had lost 75 per cent of their strength. Total German losses for the ill-starred

I cannot understand how a man like Paulus would not rather go to his death. The heroism of so many tens of thousands of men, officers and generals is nullified by such a man. What hurts me most personally is that I still promoted him to Fieldmarshal. I wanted to give him this final satisfaction. That is the last Fieldmarshal I shall appoint in this war. You must not count your chickens before they are hatched.

Caucasus and Stalingrad adventure amounted to 1,500,000 men and six months' arms production in the Reich. In the shock of this unimaginable defeat, Hitler was swept by ungenerous emotions. His immediate reaction was one of spite for the wretched Fieldmarshal Paulus who had had the effrontery to survive the debacle.

It was the hardest blow the German Army ever received and it almost sent the Fuhrer demented. For months he became a virtual recluse and ate alone, only emerging for interminable military conferences. The tide which had begun to turn against him at El Alamein in the desert in October 1942 rushed back with a vengeance in the snows of Stalingrad during January 1943.

Below: 31 *January* 1943, *Fieldmarshal Paulus surrenders.*
Opposite (top): *The Battle is over. German losses had totalled 1,500,000 men.*
Opposite (below): *Russian forces link up in the defence of Stalingrad—9.20 am, 31 January 1943.*

KURSK

KURSK WAS THE GREATEST tank battle in history. The Germans gathered the finest divisions of the Wehrmacht and the *Waffen SS*, in an enormous concentration of men and armour for a massive offensive to reverse the disaster of Stalingrad. They knew that there could be no question of failure; only a decisive victory over the Red Army could ease the relentless, threatening pressure of the Eastern front and free the Wehrmacht to deal with the Anglo-American forces which looked set for an invasion of mainland Europe.

Although Hitler had been initially shattered by the impact of the Stalingrad defeat, the brilliant generalship of Fieldmarshal Erich von Manstein snatched a glittering success from the heels of that disaster and caused the Fuhrer's hopes to revive. During February 1943, while the retreating German armies streaming back from the Caucasus looked certain to be annihilated and the Russians had hammered their way into Kharkov, only excellent leadership and the traditional steadiness of the German soldier staved off the virtual destruction of Army Group South. In March, Manstein, one of Germany's greatest operational commanders, struck back. Rapidly reorganizing his forces—which included several of the crack *Waffen SS* armoured divisions—he squeezed the Russians out of Kharkov in a complicated battle of manoeuvre. His forces were then poised to tackle the Russians, exposed in a vulnerable salient around Kursk. The spring thaw had turned the Russian roads and countryside to mud, so Manstein was unable to strike his blow towards Kursk—but his successes appeared to have wiped out the stigma of Stalingrad.

Early in March, Hitler began to appreciate both the effect and the nature of Manstein's campaign. Instead of despairing of the situation in Russia he was once again thinking of the East as the most potentially rewarding theatre of operations.

5 MARCH 1943

Space is one of the most important military factors. You can conduct military operations only if you have space. We have a battlefield in the East that has room for strategical operations.

The German Army was still better equipped and trained for a war of manoeuvre than the Red Army, and the vast spaces of the Eastern front allowed it to show its paces. Not only Hitler, but a considerable body of opinion among the German generals was beginning to feel that, if they eschewed the sort of grandiose schemes which had overstretched them in the past, they could still inflict crippling damage on the Russian Army by outmanoeuvering it in front of less distant objectives.

Although there was general agreement that some sort of offensive should be mounted against the Russians, there was considerable wrangling over the actual plan of attack. The Chief of the German General Staff, Kurt Zeitzler, was very much in favour of resuming the operations which Manstein had been forced to abandon in the spring. The Russians were reputed to have 1,000,000 men in the Kursk salient—a bulge roughly semi-circular in shape which jutted 75 miles westward into the German lines, with its base measuring more than 100 miles across. A drive through the shoulders of this salient could encircle its Russian defenders and tear an irreparable hole in the centre of the Russian front. The advantages were obvious—so obvious that they were appreciated by the Russians, who were steadily improving their defences around Kursk. Evidence of this Russian activity persuaded Manstein that the plan was no longer so likely to succeed and he opposed it.

Hitler himself was undecided about the wisdom of the Kursk plan and he summoned the operational generals from the front to rehearse arguments for and against it at his headquarters. The staff generals who were closest to Hitler, such as Zeitzler himself and Keitel, Chief of the Supreme Command, were all in favour—as was Fieldmarshal von Kluge, Commander of Army Group Centre, who would be in charge of the attack on the northern side of Kursk. Manstein was unwilling to express full-blooded opposition—possibly because he knew that Hitler, as usual, would ultimately be won over by the more enthusiastic general and press ahead regardless. The only real dissent came from a man who had not been asked for his opinion—Colonel-General Heinz Guderian, Inspector-General of Armoured Troops. Guderian was emphatically against any major operations in 1943 because he believed that Germany needed time to build up her armoured forces and should not squander them. He was also against any plan that had lost the element of surprise. Hitler realized that a major offensive would be needed to stave off the blows of the Red Army, and the weight of opinion in favour of the plan decided him. However, he did not make up his mind without grave misgivings.

10 MAY 1943

Whenever I think of this attack my stomach turns over.

The exhaustion of the German forces after their disasters in Russia and North Africa was so great that the Kursk offensive—codenamed Operation Zitadelle—could not begin until after midsummer. Guderian and Reich's Armaments Minister Speer were at last getting a healthy production flow of tanks and other war material, but it took some time before the Panzer divisions on which so much depended could be brought up to something approaching establishment level in equipment. As a bonus they were mostly being issued with a new main battle tank—the Panther D—an extremely fine AFV which could at least match the Russian T34 but which showed the inevitable teething troubles of a brand new model during the first months of its use. Still uncertain about the plan, Hitler postponed Zitadelle from 13 June to the beginning of July so that an extra couple of battalions of Panthers would be ready for it. Just before the battle he was reassuring his generals and, possibly, himself that it was necessary because any retreat from the occupied territories in Russia was unthinkable.

1 JULY 1943

The blame for our misfortunes must be laid squarely on our allies. Germany needs the conquered territories or she will not exist for long. She must win hegemony over the rest of Europe. Where we are we stay.

One way and another the Germans had assembled an awesome array of force. Colonel-General Model's Ninth Army with seven Panzer, two Panzergrenadier and nine infantry divisions was to attack from the north. Colonel-General Hoth's Fourth Panzer Army with ten Panzer, one Panzergrenadier and seven infantry divisions would sweep up from the south. Opposing the 36 German divisions were 11 Russian Armies (each roughly equivalent to a German Corps) which had been carefully disposed to counter the German onslaught. The shoulders of the salient had been densely sown with mines, and the bulk of the Russian troops had been withdrawn from the head of the bulge to be ready for counter-attack. Among their 20,000 guns, the Russians had no less than 6,000 anti-tank guns and they had swarms of their rugged T34 tanks. As far as they could they had made Kursk into a trap for the Germans but, although they knew that the Russians were waiting for them, German morale was reported to be high. No doubt the German soldiers believed that the sheer weight of their assault would be unstoppable. The armoured spearheads also contained a high proportion of the fanatical, dedicated *Waffen SS*— the southern pincer included the celebrated SS Panzer Corps with the divisions *Leibstandarte Adolf Hitler*, *Totenkopf* (Death's Head) and *Das Reich* besides the

super-Panzer-grenadier formation of *Gross Deutschland*. These, if any, were fervently determined to show the world that resistance to them was hopeless.

4 JULY 1943

This day the soldiers of the Reich are to take part in an offensive of such importance that the whole future of the war may depend on its outcome. More than anything else, victory will show the whole world that resistance to the power of the German Army is hopeless.

Their ardour was not dampened by the four-hour artillery bombardment with which the Russians preceded the offensive to show that they were well aware of what was about to happen. Yet the German advance did not go with its usual dash. The Russian preparations had been too thorough, and the Panzers had to slog slowly forward taking steady losses. In a symbolic incident on 7 July the SS division *Gross Deutschland* had its way forward blocked by a mass of Soviet tanks so that, for several hours, 500 tanks simply faced each other and blasted away until nightfall. The wastage of this sort of warfare was huge and little ground was gained. Where the Germans did take a position easily they usually found that it was an ambush and that Russian guns were carefully zeroed in on it to bring down a destructive barrage. Although the Luftwaffe provided superb ground support for their armoured units, it failed to protect the German rail links from Red Air Force bombers so that supplies of ammunition began to dwindle. After a week of action the German spearhead formations were showing signs of exhaustion and had made only piecemeal advances.

To add to German problems, the Red Army was on the offensive just north and south of the salient so that the infantry divisions were busy resisting them rather than assisting the Panzers. There were rumours of heavier Russian offensives at other places along the whole extended Eastern front, so that it was obvious that the Germans would have to conclude their Kursk operation quickly and redeploy their armoured units to meet these new threats. On 12 July, Hoth summoned the Corps commanders of the southern pincer and instructed them to go for a knockout blow. He used all 600 operative tanks for the attack which has become famous as 'The Death Ride of Fourth Panzer Army'. The great columns of German tanks were counter-attacked by the full weight of the fresh Russian Fifth Armoured Army and the superior range of weight of the guns mounted on the German Tiger and Panther tanks was nullified by the blinding dust and shortage of ammunition. Each side lost more than 300 tanks on the battlefield, losses which the Germans could afford far less than the Russians.

As his picked troops were decimated in this unsubtle battle between armoured masses, Hitler failed to realize that the strength of his forces was being permanently sapped. On 12 July the Allies had landed in Sicily, but Hitler refused to contemplate trying to make peace with the Soviets to be able to deal with this new menace. He was the only leader with the genius to attain all the conquests Germany needed to establish her New Order in the world. The defeat of Russia would have to be completed in his lifetime, so his forces must fight on whatever the cost.

Obediently the German Army continued its struggle in the cauldron of Kursk although the battle was clearly lost. The first Russian summer offensive of the war had been launched and had broken through as far as the rear echelons of the SS Corps, which was still struggling to implement Operation Zitadelle. In the north, the Red Army had taken Orel—a German forward position that had threatened Moscow since 1941 and which was of proven strength. The fall of Orel was a great psychological blow, for it freed the Russians from fear for Moscow and it removed a bastion which had been as important to the Germans as Tobruk had been to the British. The pincers around Kursk had never reduced the Russian held base of the salient to a dangerously thin corridor—it had always been at least 60 miles wide. Now that the German spearheads were actually being forced back it was only accepting reality to cancel the operation.

For once in his life, Hitler seemed prepared to abandon an offensive without too much reluctance. The truth was that his heart had never been in the Kursk plan, and it may well be that he had no realization of how much it had cost him, or that its verdict was final.

The aftermath of Kursk was made all the more serious for the German armed forces by the fact that, for once, Hitler's attention was fatally distracted from the Eastern front. Twenty Panzer divisions had been bled white, but there was some hope in the East if they could be quickly re-equipped and used in counter-attacks to stem the Russian onslaught. But Hitler was pre-occupied with Italy—not so much because of the activities of the Western Allies but because he suspected that the Italians were preparing to revoke their alliance with Germany. In Hitler's mean-minded view, revenge for 'treachery' always took precedence over military good sense. The counter-offensive and holding operations in the East would have to be abandoned until he had dealt the Italians a blow that would send them reeling.

This meant that the Germans lost the initiative in the East and never regained it. In Operation Zitadelle their last grand attack had been blunted, and the demands of new fronts opening up in the West ensured that they would never again have an offensive capacity in the East. By December 1943 the reconstituted Ninth and Fourth Panzer Armies had been pushed back to the Dneiper and beyond. The whole of the Eastern front from Nevel in the north to Kirovograd in the south reflected the turning of the tide.

Below: *Kursk resulted in Germany losing over 300 tanks.*

NORMANDY

AS 1943 DREW TO A CLOSE, the Thousand Year Reich founded by Hitler was running very short of political and military capital. The last major German victory of the war, which had been won at Kharkov in March, had long since been overwhelmingly reversed by the progress of the Red Army's first summer offensive. The Western Allies were slogging up the Italian peninsular and, although the nature of the terrain prevented them from exerting a crippling pressure on the German defence, it was obvious that they held the initiative in the Mediterranean theatre. Added to this grim scenario was the knowledge that an Allied invasion through the West Wall of *Festung Europa* (fortress Europe) had been long promised and would certainly materialize. Yet there was no dread of the impending invasion among the German people, their military leaders or their Fuhrer; on the contrary, it seemed to offer them their only ray of hope.

5 NOVEMBER   **1943**

When the enemy invades in the West it will be the moment of decision in this war, and the moment must turn to our advantage. We must ruthlessly extract every ounce of effort from Germany.

Hitler was perfectly well aware that the invasion would present his forces with a crucial test and that its outcome might well decide the war. There were however certain factors dominating the timing of the invasion which worked very much in favour of the overstretched defending armies. There was no danger of an invasion being undertaken across the rough winter seas, so Hitler was able to use all his available forces to gain a breathing space on the other fronts—hoping they might then remain stable when troops were withdrawn in the spring to meet the promised Allied landings. As he made perfectly clear, the defeat of the Anglo-American invasion in the West was his top priority for which he was prepared to 'ruthlessly extract every ounce of effort from Germany'. It presented him with the opportunity of dealing a quick and telling blow that would devastate his Western opponents and leave him free to concentrate the full might of his forces, backed by the resources of occupied Europe, upon the Eastern front.

Right: *D-day. The first wave of invasion troops came from the air, but, despite the Germans' unpreparedness, the Allies did not have an easy time—particularly on Omaha, where American units suffered appalling casualties.*

20 DECEMBER   **1943**

There is no doubt that the attack in the West will come in the spring. The whole problem of the West has to be carefully considered. I am constantly thinking of new ways to improve the defence. Automatic flamethrowers for instance, and oil cans that can be thrown in the sea and then begin to burn. In case of a landing we could also burn or blow up barrels on the beach so that they would have to wade through fire.

During the crucial winter of 1943-44, the Fuhrer exercised his undoubted genius for detail on arranging a murderous reception for the Anglo-American assault waves. As Hitler never ceased to remind his listeners, he had been a front line soldier during World War I. During that static conflict the science of defence had been lethally refined to a pitch of excellence which Hitler was determined to excel when he fortified the western coasts of subjugated Europe. He delighted in schemes which would make any landing so difficult that the actual inter-

vention of German troops would be almost unnecessary. To this end, he harnessed industrial production to the manufacture of defensive weaponry to beef up a barrier which he boastingly named his Atlantic Wall.

During March 1944, the pace of activity quickened as the likely date of invasion neared and it became necessary to make more detailed counter-invasion plans. The whole western theatre of operations was under the command of Germany's senior Fieldmarshal, Gerd von Rundstedt, who discharged his responsibilities by setting up his headquarters in Paris's most luxurious hotel—the George V— and spending much of his time in the dynamic study of detective novels. In charge of the defences and of the battle for the beaches themselves was one of Hitler's favourites—Fieldmarshal Erwin Rommel. Rommel was a moody character, prone to bouts of despair, but even his enemies (who were mostly to be found among senior German soldiers) admitted that he had immense ability, even a touch of genius. With the German public he was a popular hero, and his British enemies considered him hardly inferior to Napoleon in military skill. The Americans, who had suffered at his hands during his bold stroke at the Kasserine pass, were equally in awe of him. To prepare for the invasion, Rommel added to his reputation for courage and distinction by showing astonishing energy and activity in deepening and strengthening the fortifications of the Atlantic Wall.

One of the reasons for Rommel's selection as the com-

mander of the anti-invasion forces was that he knew all about fighting the British. This was all the more important in that the German intelligence operation in Britain was negligible; an informed guess as to the actual site of the landings was the best that the Germans could hope for. Rommel reckoned that the shores of Holland and Belgium were too easily defensible through flooding to be considered and, of all places south, he favoured the area around the Pas de Calais and the mouth of the Somme. He knew that the Channel crossing was a major and frightening undertaking and he believed that the British were bound, on previous form, to take the militarily correct objective of the shortest crossing point and to use their long suit of stubborness and brute force to hammer their way ashore. He felt that the Normandy beaches were too far from effective fighter cover and that the lesson of Anzio had shown that they would not be bold enough to risk operating without an air umbrella. He knew little of the Americans but believed that they would follow the British lead.

Despite all these arguments, Hitler's intuition led him to contradict Rommel. He was in possession of the reports of the spy 'Cicero' who operated in the British Embassy at Istanbul and these indicated a Normandy landing zone.

Opposite: *Montgomery speaks to his troops during preparations for the Normandy landings.*

Left: *Eisenhower with an American airborne division— whose job would be to paralyze German communications just prior to the landings.*

I consider Normandy and Brittany to be particularly threatened by invasion because they are very suitable for the creation of beachheads.

The Fuhrer had little confidence in 'Cicero' as he could not understand why the British should need to tell their ambassador to Turkey of their planning details, but he recognized that Normandy and Brittany offered favourable conditions for creating sheltered beach-heads. As a result of his urging, Rommel unwillingly turned his formidable energies to building the Atlantic Wall in the Normandy-Brittany peninsular. By the spring, Rommel's best-guess area of the Pas de Calais was the most heavily fortified stretch of the Atlantic coast—Normandy and Brittany came a good second.

The preparations for the invasion also involved the vexed question of the best way to dispose the defending armies. To meet the invasion, Rundstedt's command would have the immense strength of 58 divisions of which 10 were Panzer divisions. For all their material strength, the Allies only had the landing craft for an initial assault by six divisions, together with three airborne, and it would take at least a week to double the number put ashore. Obviously the Germans held all the strong cards if they could bring their might to bear quickly at the point of invasion. Rommel, who knew what he was up against, wanted to spread his less mobile forces along the coast to contest the beaches themselves and he wanted the Panzers dispersed immediately behind the coastline so that some of them at least would be very quickly into action. Unfortunately Rommel's ideas were hotly opposed by the dashing group of Panzer commanders which had been responsible for so much German military success.

The most important of these was General Baron Leo Geyr von Schweppenburg, who was in command of the Panzer divisions in France. He wished to hold the Panzers well back from the coast and wait until the Allies advanced from their bridgehead before destroying them in a war of movement. He was supported by the brilliant Colonel-General Heinz Guderian, Inspector-General of Armoured Forces, who was always adamantly opposed to committing Panzers piecemeal and believed in combining them for one mighty blow. Despite their abilities, both Geyr and Guderian were ignorant of the realities of massive Anglo-American air superiority. Rommel knew the British methods well, and furiously explained to Geyr that his mobile forces would be rendered totally immobile by day and largely immobile by night in the face of rocket-firing fighter-bombers, cratered roads and bombed bridges. He also knew his enemies' stubborness and declared that if the invaders had not been driven back into the sea within four days they never would be.

In this clash of wills, Guderian and Rommel both appealed to Hitler for backing. Hitler was temperamentally more in tune with Rommel's ideas of absolute

A giant gun emplacement on the Atlantic Wall.
The Pas de Calais was the area most strongly defended

resistance on the beaches and he gave cautious backing to the forward deployment of the Panzers. However, to make the worst of both worlds, he agreed to set up a Panzer reserve of a few divisions which would remain under his personal control. Rommel, who was after all a particularly bold tank commander himself, was infuriated at this dilution of his command and dismayed that his fellow soldiers had so little idea of the storm that they would have to face.

Hitler's decision to maintain a Panzer reserve was all the more pointless in that he had begun to endorse Rommel's attitude to the anti-invasion strategy by the end of March.

20 MARCH   **1944**

Obviously an Anglo-American invasion in the West is going to come. The most suitable landing areas and hence those that are in the most danger are the two west-coast peninsulars of Cherbourg and Brest. They offer very tempting possibilities for the creation of bridgeheads which could be enlarged thereafter by the massive use of air power. The enemy's invasion operation must not, under any circumstances, be allowed to survive longer than hours or, at most, days. Once defeated, the enemy will never again try to invade.

It is clear that Hitler's ideas were fully formed and that he held to a coherent and rational plan for the defence of *Festung Europa*. He differed from Rommel only in his conviction that the Norman-Breton coast offered the most likely scope for the assault, but he was well aware of the power of Allied air superiority. He concurred absolutely with the principle that the Allies must be driven back into the sea before they could establish a secure beach-head, and indulged in great hopes of a definitive German victory. He was always contemptuous of democracies and he believed that a thwarted invasion would leave the Western Allies with a political crisis which would force them out of the war. He even believed that Roosevelt might end up in jail if the American electorate turned against him.

As the crucial year dragged into April both Rommel and Hitler became increasingly optimistic. Rommel had done so much work on the Atlantic Wall, and he had such powerful forces at his disposal, that his confidence grew as the quantity of mine-laying and barrier building reached a crescendo. The Fuhrer, sniffing suspiciously at the intelligence reports that reached him, believed that the Allies were bluffing. He began to hope that there would be no second front and that the Anglo-Americans were so

frightened by the German preparations that they would not press the war *à l'outrance*.

6 APRIL   **1944**

The whole way the British are serving all this up to us looks phoney. This latest news about the restrictions they are ordering, their security clamp-down and so on—now you do not go in for all that if you are really up to something. I cannot help feeling that the whole thing is going to turn out to be a shameless charade.

In fact, Hitler was right to smell a rat but wrong to believe that he would escape the breaching of his Atlantic Wall. The Allies were engaged in a deception which was intended to rivet German attention on the Pas de Calais area even after the Normandy beach-heads were a fact. To this end they ordered a security clamp-down when the tides were right for an assault around Calais and re-inforced German misconceptions by bombing bridges north of the Seine. They also established 25 mythical divisions around the very real person of their most feared tank exponent, US Lieutenant-General George S. Patton Jnr. Until Patton actually appeared in Normandy, long after the beach-heads were secured, large German forces were kept around the Pas de Calais to fend him off.

So infectious was the air of optimism that, when the vast Allied invasion fleet steamed out of the misty dawn of 6 June and started setting the first wave ashore, the German commanders were totally unprepared. Rommel was at his home in Germany, many of the divisional commanders for the Normandy-Brittany sector were away from their divisions at an exercise in Brittany and Hitler was asleep. In answer to frantic telephone calls, Rommel came hurrying back—but Hitler's staff refused to wake the Fuhrer or to authorise the use of the Panzer reserve, still believing that the real invasion would come in the Pas de Calais. When Hitler awoke he obviously agreed with his staff's assessment, for he issued orders for the immediate eradication of the beach-head and laid stress on the fact that further landings could be expected.

Despite the Germans' unpreparedness, the Allies did not have an easy time. Under the command of Montgomery, they landed on five beaches. Two American and one British airborne divisions were dropped inland to paralyze German communications and help the assault troops on to their more distant objectives. It is still impossible to establish exactly what the immediate strategic aims of the invasion were, owing to the quarrels, faulty memories and downright mendacity of the senior Allied generals, but it is fair to assume that simply getting ashore was top priority. This was quickly achieved everywhere except at Omaha beach where the defences proved very difficult to destroy, and there was much confusion owing to the eastward drift of the tide. The American units disembarked there suffered appalling casualties and, despite many displays of doggedness and courage, they might never have breached their section of the Atlantic Wall if Allied successes to right and left of them had not distracted the defence. It showed that Rommel's plan to hold the beaches was workable where the defenders were ready.

By the evening of 6 June the battle for the beaches had been lost by the Germans, and the hopes of both Hitler and Rommel had been dashed. After this, German strategy would have to rely on denying the Allies their objectives and gradually making their position impossible. From the position of the landings it seemed clear to Hitler that the Americans had the vital task of securing a port—probably Cherbourg—and the British (who had landed their crack 7th Armoured Division) were to push south to cut off the defenders of the Breton peninsular. Field-marshal Montgomery often denied later that this was his plan, but he certainly acted as though it was at the time.

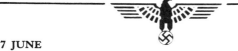

17 JUNE   **1944**

The Cherbourg fortress is to hold out as long as possible—if possible until mid-July. The time is not ripe for a political decision yet. Normandy is not to be spoken of as 'the enemy's bridgehead' but as 'the last piece of enemy-occupied France'. The enemy will not last out the summer. They have already committed all their battle-experienced divisions to Normandy which suggests that they have their hands full.

Hitler realized that the most important move was to deny the enemy a port; it would be extraordinarily difficult to supply the Allied armies across open beaches at the mercy of the rough Atlantic weather. He refused to accept that the Anglo-American forces were established on the continent and instructed Rommel and Rundstedt to keep them bottled up.

As Hitler read it all, the major battles of the war in Europe and North Africa had been decided by encirclement. His partial success in France in May 1940, his sweeping victories in Russia in 1941 as well as his defeats at Stalingrad and in Tunisia had all been occasioned by cutting the losing forces from their supply lines. He realized that the great defensive strength of the Anglo-Americans meant that it was unlikely that he could counter-attack them with success but, if he could hold them in check, he might achieve their encirclement by interrupting their supply columns across the broad Atlantic.

29 JUNE   **1944**

We have got to lay mines and still more mines in the Seine bay with the tenacity of a bulldog. It is incomparably more effective to sink a ship's whole cargo than to have to fight the unloaded personnel and material separately on land at a later date. We can nourish the battle only if we manage to get our own supplies through and that means that the navy, air force and our own domestic economy turn over every modern truck they have to the army transport convoys. Then, if everything goes well, perhaps we can launch a counter-attack on the Americans after all.

Hitler hoped that intensive mine laying would weaken the invading forces and cause them to wither on the vine. He was also very aware that the heavy Allied air superiority amounted to a threat to strangle his own supply lines, and he prepared vigorous action to clear them. If all went well, the strength of the Allies would be sapped and the German strength increased until he could counter-attack.

The Fuhrer did not contemplate a completely static defensive during the period of waiting for the balance to tilt in his favour. His V-weapons had been raining down on London since early June, and he was so convinced that they were having a devastating effect that he believed that the enemy commanders would be forced to mount an offensive on their launching sites in northern France.

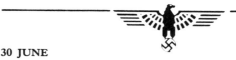

30 JUNE   **1944**

The enemy has been forced to move because of our V-weapon operations. What matters now is to wear them down by gunfire and by slinging rapid punches at every opportunity. Caen will be the main pivot of the enemy thrust towards Paris. So we have got to pack more and more forces into the line there.

Hitler meant to be ready for what he imagined to be an offensive provoked by desperation, and he rightly guessed that it would come in the area around Caen. He surely had enough troops and equipment on the spot to deny Caen to his enemies and hold them on a line Caen-Avranches. Although his picked divisions were suffering severely in the defensive fighting, he was adamant that there could be no question of retreat.

I flatly forbid any withdrawal from Caen. The present lines are to be held. All further enemy penetrations are to be stopped by determined defence or by limited counter-attacks.

Once again Hitler's instincts seem to have been right—although Montgomery often denied that he meant to make a breakthrough at Caen. The fact is that Caen was almost annihilated by an exceptional carpet-bombing on 18 July and the German positions around it were attacked by the massed array of three British Armoured Divisions. Thanks to Hitler's foresight and Rommel's care in preparing positions of unguessed at strength and depth, the British made a deep penetration but not a break-

Below: *Simply getting ashore was the top priority—an objective quickly achieved everywhere except at Omaha beach. There, the American troops might never have breached their section of the Atlantic Wall had it not been for Allied successes on either side of them.*

through. However, the Germans did not possess the strength to hold off British attacks of such power and place equally impregnable defences in front of the Americans. Matters were made worse for them by the fact that Rommel had been badly wounded in an air attack on 17 July and could take no further part in the battle. On 31 July the US First Army managed to make a breach at Avranches, and Patton—now in Normandy—sent his Third Army flooding through.

With Patton on the loose, the German position was desperate. The forces which had so long held the line from Caen to Avranches were pinned between the Americans and the British in the Falaise gap and all but annihilated. By the end of August the German armies in the West had collapsed. Paris was liberated; Patton's armoured hordes swept eastwards while the British spearhead of the Guards Armoured Division was covering 75 miles a day in its drive for Belgium. Looking back, Hitler realized that his defeat around Falaise was the worst blow he had ever received. He also criticised Rommel, not for the first time, for pessimism, but still expressed his admiration for the Fieldmarshal's military ability. However, when the Gestapo unearthed a rather tenuous connection between Rommel and the Stauffenberg plot, the SS were sent on 14 October to force that most gallant and upright of soldiers to commit suicide.

THE ARDENNES

HITLER WAS ALWAYS A PASSIONATE advocate of the offensive as the only way to win, so it should have been obvious, when the Fuhrer had his back to the wall in December 1944, he would counter-attack. But the Allies were flushed with success; their intelligence was misreading the German dispositions; and there were serious divisions between American and British soldiers on how the war should be finished off quickly. Although the British Fieldmarshal Montgomery wanted all available supplies allocated to his Anglo-American Army Group so that it could spearhead a swift dash for the Ruhr, his commander, General Dwight Eisenhower, believed that all the Allied armies in the West should move forward together. Eisenhower's plan meant an enforced pause for resupply along the whole front.

Hitler's plan for a grand-slam in December 1944 owed something to the successful Panzer thrust which had laid France low in 1940. Once again he thought that a surprise punch through the Ardennes and a northward hook behind the Allies left wing would bring a decisive victory. The 1944 edition of this scheme was only slightly less ambitious than its predecessor, and the German armies were still expected to force a crossing of the Meuse. The only concession to the comparative German weakness of 1944 was that the blow was aimed short of the Channel ports, but was still intended to reach Antwerp—a seaport vital to the Allies with its capacity to support 50 divisions.

This gambler's throw was absolutely bound to fail—even the German generals leading it were sure of that. It was true that the Allied lines in the Ardennes were lightly garrisoned, but there were excellent reasons for that: the best being that the heavily wooded and hilly countryside was totally unsuited for the deployment of armoured forces or any large forces. There was no significant off-road capacity even for tanks in this area; the Panzers would have no chance to roll happily round strongpoints encircling their defenders—they would have to take every defended crossroads. The general lack of roads through the Ardennes meant considerable congestion and a jammed tailback behind the armoured spearheads which would prove highly vulnerable in the face of Allied air superiority. All this had been overcome in 1940 because the French and the BEF did not have a single armoured division to counter the surprise breakthrough; in 1944, the Anglo-American armies were dripping with armoured formations, and even their infantry divisions were mechanized.

On a straightforward assessment it was a lunatic scheme, but Hitler was relying on other than purely military considerations. As Guderian, Chief of the German General Staff, later observed, the Fuhrer lived in a special world and the realities had to be bent to conform with his preferred outlook. He had consistently derided the fighting ability of the American soldier (mainly because he was terrified of admitting to himself the massive power of the US) and he was always trying to convince himself that the British had taken so much punishment that they were about to quit. He had secretly assembled two Panzer Armies containing 10 Panzer and 17 motorized divisions with a total of 2000 tanks and 250,000 men. This concentration of power could deliver a heavy offensive blow and, as Hitler read it, this should produce enough panic in the Americans and defeatism in the British to drive home to its objective. He even believed that this reverse could drive some of his opponents out of the war. He was no simpleton where political interests were concerned and he reckoned that, by lashing out, he could put the unlikely coalition of his enemies under strain.

12 DECEMBER   **1944**

America tries to become England's heir; Russia tries to gain the Balkans. Even now these states are at loggerheads. If now we can deliver a few more blows, then at any moment this artificially bolstered common front may suddenly collapse with a gigantic clap of thunder. It is essential to deprive the enemy of his belief that victory is certain.

Overall command had been vested in Fieldmarshal Gerd von Rundstedt—an amiable slacker who conducted most of his campaigns in the role of detached observer—while the battlefront commander was Fieldmarshal Walther Model, a brilliant, committed soldier with an amazing record of snatching victory from defeat. Each of the two Panzer Armies was to be led by soldiers of proven dash and brilliance. The Fifth Panzer Army was led by the 47-year-old innovative General Hasso von Manteuffel and the Sixth SS Panzer Army (the first SS Army formation of the war) by Colonel-General Joseph 'Sepp' Dietrich, Hitler's ex-chauffeur—a rough, vigorous man who had proved his worth in all the major campaigns of the war.

Under the complex system of command which distinguished the Third Reich, the direction of the war in the West was kept quite separate from that in the East. Guderian regarded the whole scheme in the West as an irresponsible adventure which jeopardized his chances of stopping the Russian steamroller, and he would have been even more concerned if he had learned of the detailed

Above: *Christmas* 1944 *in the Ardennes—
Hitler's last, short-lived success.*

plans for the opening of the offensive. OKW's rather unoriginal idea was that the breakthrough should be achieved by infantry divisions and then exploited by the Panzers who would pour through the ready-made gap. Guderian had spent most of the war stressing that armoured divisions should always form the assault spearhead and that infantry divisions only got in their way; and it can be assumed that Manteuffel and Dietrich agreed with this general idea. However, it was immensely difficult to prevail upon OKW to make any alterations to their plan—although Manteuffel succeeded in getting permission to use his infantry to infiltrate the American positions rather than to storm them.

The pessimism of the German commanders was kept from the troops, and Rundstedt recorded that morale was surprisingly high. So the usual dash was much in evidence when both Panzer Armies struck on 16 December on a 40 mile front. Surprise was complete and the Allies were taken off balance. Half a dozen American divisions were rolled up, encircled or over-run—even army headquarters were forced to pack up and run for it. The idea that the

war in Europe was practically all over bar the shouting took a knock as flying bombs began raining down out of the winter fog and jeeploads of SS commandos in American uniforms spread confusion behind the lines. The overcast weather kept the Allied air forces on the ground, and there was pandemonium as the Panzers stormed forward and the SS showed their usual form in murdering scores of American prisoners.

Eisenhower, as Supreme Commander, however, was quick to take the necessary measures to stem the flood. He was helped in this by the extraordinary courage and endurance of isolated American units which hung on to vital positions long after they had lost touch with their headquarters behind them. This meant that although the Germans had reached Stavelot on the 17th and were only 15 miles from the important road junction of Bastogne on the morning of the 18th, they were not moving as fast and freely as they seemed to be. On the night of the 17th the 101st US Airborne Division was rushed 100 miles from its reserve position at Reims into Bastogne just ahead of Manteuffel's spearhead.

At the same time, Eisenhower sorted out the snags of a confused command. He put Montgomery in command north of the German breakthrough and US General

Omar N. Bradley in charge to the south. 'Monty' has had his critics but no one ever denied that he was a superb organizer—he had been showing his skills in that direction ever since May 1940—and he pushed an Anglo-American Corps between the Germans and the Meuse in no time. While the British Fieldmarshal was sewing up the defences against the proposed hook north, Bradley was organizing a counter-attack against the southern edge of the bulge made by the German salient. The Allies only had two tank commanders with the boldness and flair which so many German Panzer leaders showed, and only one of them was in command of an army. He was the towering larger-than-life Lieutenant General George S. Patton Jnr., a hard-driving US cavalryman whose Third Army was planning a Christmas attack on the Saar. When he was asked to switch his offensive northward, the irrepressible Patton managed to get his first three divisions into position in 72 hours. In no time, his troops were grinding into the southern flank of the Panzer thrust.

For a while, neither side was very happy about the progress of the battle. The Germans surrounded Bastogne but could not end the stubborn resistance of the garrison. This meant that communication with their spearheads was severely restricted, and they put in heavy attacks on the beleaguered 101st Airborne. The Allied commanders were alarmed by the extent of German successes which had expanded the Bulge until its right shoulder rested on Malmedy and its tip was not far short of the Meuse at Celles.

The vital date was 23 December; the skies cleared and the combined fleets of the RAF and the Eighth American Air Force took to the air to give the long road-bound German columns a hammering. By the following day Manteuffel reckoned that he had got as far as he was going and an apoplectic Guderian turned up at the Fuhrer's headquarters to warn him about an immense offensive being prepared by the Red Army. He begged Hitler to switch his Panzer Armies from West to East. Unfortunately, the Ardennes project was dear to Hitler's heart and he was in no mood to listen to reason. He dismissed all the carefully compiled figures of Russian strength as so much rubbish and convinced himself that his Western opponents were crumbling.

24 DECEMBER   **1944**

It's the greatest imposture since Genghis Khan. Who is responsible for producing all this rubbish?

The factors which had held the Germans back made the counter-offensive hard going for Patton. The Ardennes were not good tank country and German defence was as stubborn as the American. Patton was not happy with the slow progress and he was fairly direct about it to his subordinate commanders: 'There's too much piddling around. Press on and get the tanks through', he said. His

Below: *A US firing squad executes two Germans from a specially formed unit which infiltrated American lines dressed in US uniform.*

American Sherman tanks, at last grouped for the counter-
offensive which came with the change in the weather and the
return of air cover.

men slogged on over Christmas Day and, on the 26th his 4th Armoured broke through to the heroic defenders of Bastogne.

28 DECEMBER   **1944**

The enemy has had to abandon all his plans for attack. He has had to throw in units that were fatigued. His operational plans have been completely upset. As much as I may be tormented by worries, nothing will make the slightest change in my decision to fight on till at last the scales tip to our side. We shall then smash the Americans completely. Then we shall see what happens. I do not believe that in the long run the enemy will be able to resist 45 German divisions. We shall yet master fate.

While Patton was giving the German left flank a mauling, the US 2nd Armoured Division was leading a fight back from the north of the Bulge. As the German generals saw it, the time had come to cut their losses and pull out before their units were cut off by the advancing Allied forces. Their opinion was not endorsed by their Fuhrer who reckoned that the offensive had been a limited success which might bring major results if it was followed up. As Hitler saw the situation, the Ardennes blow had focused Allied attention around it and brought American and British units scurrying from all over the front to deal with it. By fighting on in the Bulge, his Panzers could keep these Allied concentrations of force busy and even overcome them while he delivered a couple of telling thrusts at other, weakened points of the line. He told his startled generals that the situation had been 'completely transformed' and made plans for eight divisions to take the offensive against Patton's army in the Saar. This was to be followed by an attack on French and American forces in Alsace masterminded by the untried military genius of Heinrich Himmler, Reichsfuhrer SS.

Despite Hitler's fiery exhortations, there was considerable pessimism among his generals, and this spread to the troops as the fighting became bitter and static. The weather closed in again, so the Germans were rid of the attentions of the Allied air forces, but the Americans were proving to be disturbingly tough opponents in a toe to toe struggle. Villages changed hands more than once, men froze to death in the bitter, winter weather and the Panzers' supplies of fuel dried up. Montgomery's forces from the north and Bradley's from the south inched forward so that all hope of German victory faded.

The Allied forces went over to the offensive in the new year, and Hitler's attacks in the Saar and Alsace came to nothing. Because of the conditions, which featured deep snowdrifts and ice-bound roads, the Allies' progress was far from spectacular. In fact the Battle of the Bulge was less of an Allied victory than a German defeat. It ended on 16 January 1945 when the Germans had been pushed back to their starting point. Neither side had gained any territory from it, but its true significance lay in the price paid. The Allies lost 80,000, mostly American, troops and the Germans 110,000. Even that disparity, however, disguises the enormity of the German loss. The reality was that Hitler had invested all his decisive military strength in the venture—the precious armoured and mechanized divisions which would never be replaced—and it had been blunted.

Left: *The enormity of the German loss was reflected not in the number of men captured or killed, but in the destruction of the precious armoured and mechanized divisions which could never be replaced.*

THE ATLANTIC

IN THE FINAL ANALYSIS, the war in Europe was decided in only three battles. The epic clashes of armies in the fall of France or at Stalingrad and El Alamein were, for all their drama, simply indicators of the relative strengths of the antagonists.

In the East, the decisive battle was the German defeat outside Moscow in December 1941—ensuring that Russia would live to fight on and develop the strength to finally crush the invading armies. In the West, defeat was made inevitable by the German failure to destroy Britain— allowing the British to build up their strength, and leaving a European base for the United States. The Fuhrer had two chances to bring the British down: the first was lost in the Battle of Britain, but the second— which occurred during the long-drawnout Battle of the Atlantic—was a much nearer and more desperate affair than either the British or German people knew at the time.

Both sides had long been aware of Britain's vulnerability. Not only did she have to import the raw materials necessary for the production of armaments, but also much of her food—so any loss of control over the sea lanes would have brought a quick end to the struggle. Luckily for the British, the position of their island—lying like a long breakwater across the North Sea—meant that the Germans were forced to use two comparatively narrow exits for their warships to the open seas: the English Channel or the route around the north of the Islands which was made doubly difficult by the presence of the main fleet at Scapa Flow and a British base on Iceland. This situation virtually denied German surface ships much hope of reaching the Atlantic, and restricted even the U-boats until the momentous events of 1940.

Below: *The destruction of one of Germany's most famous 'pocket' battleships, the* Graf Spee.

If the Norwegian campaign had failed we should not have been able to create the conditions which were a pre-requisite for the success of our submarines. Without the coast of Norway at our disposal we should not have been able to launch our attacks against the ports of the Midlands and Northern Britain and operations in the Arctic waters would also have been impracticable.

In April 1942, when the Germans seemed to be winning the Battle of the Atlantic, Hitler looked back to the invasion of Norway as the cause of his success—but his success against France was just as important. From

Below: *A convoy in mid-Atlantic. 1942 was the year of peak achievement for the U-boat. In both February and March, U-boats sunk 500,000 tons of Allied shipping, and 700,000 tons in June.*

Norway, his ships could dart out to round Iceland and reach the Atlantic without making the long journey up the North Sea in the full glare of British observation. From bases south of Calais, German warships were already beyond the most constricting part of the Channel—they only had to leave harbour to be in the Atlantic.

The Germans had not been idle before the fall of France, but their Navy had never threatened to win the war single-handed. Surface raiders such as the famous 'pocket battleships' *Graf Spee* and *Deutschland* had achieved some small successes, however, before being hunted from the oceans, and the U-boats had struck very hard if one considers that there were only 56 of them at the outbreak of war. U.47 had even penetrated the defences of Scapa Flow and sunk the battleship *Royal Oak*, but the swift introduction of the convoy system had a deterrent effect.

After the conquest of France and Norway, the Germans were soon able to inflict a crisis level of shipping losses on the British. The neutrality of the Irish Free State worked decisively in the German favour as the range of air cover was the most important factor in affording protection to the convoys. All shipping had to be routed around the north of Ireland and the south-western approaches abandoned. Even that last life-line was threatened by

the Germans, in three ways—with long-range bombers, with surface ships and, most of all, with U-boats.

The long-range bomber was the four-engined Focke-Wulf 'Kondor' (FW200), which could prescribe a long arc out over the Atlantic from a base at Merignac near Bordeaux to another at Stavanger in Norway. On these great looping flights, the 'Kondor' could keep out of range of British air cover and make effective low-level bombing runs on the largely unprotected convoys of 1940. In October alone, Kondors sank 66,000 tons of shipping. Unfortunately for the Germans, the Kondors only achieved their extreme range by being very lightly constructed and carrying huge amounts of fuel—so they were unable to absorb much punishment. Increasing AA protection for British merchant ships, together with the introduction of catapult fired Hurricane fighters on ship decks, ended the Kondor menace.

German surface ships were a more enduring threat to Britain's sea lanes than the Kondor. Although the capital ships could best be used after 'Barbarossa' in threatening the British Arctic Convoys from Norwegian ports, they also made a number of forays into the Atlantic. On most occasions there was nothing to protect the British convoys from this sort of weighty opposition but, on two occasions, the desperate and doomed resistance of

a single British armed merchant cruiser drove immensely more powerful German forces away from their prey. This was a tribute not only to the gallantry of the Royal Navy but to the German need to conserve their few capital units. Any damage which resulted in a loss of speed or manoeuvrability would leave them at the mercy of the incomparably more powerful Royal Navy—which could send irresistable forces hurrying after a foe too crippled to slip away from them. This was exactly what happened to the great German battleship *Bismarck* in May 1941, and her loss prompted even greater caution from the German Navy. After all, a capital ship in harbour still tied up powerful British forces ready to oppose her.

Hitler had an ambiguous attitude towards employment of large warships. On the one hand he did not like losing them; on the other he was scornful of his Navy's caution. In the end, he dismissed any ideas of using capital ships successfully and even threatened on 6 January 1943 to have them all broken up and their guns used for coastal defence.

19 JUNE   **1943**

Evolution these days has been so swift that it is now the infantry of the seas which assumes the prime importance. Apart from submarines our greatest need is for little ships…powerful corvettes, destroyers and the like…these are the classes that carry on the fight.
The Japanese today possess the most powerful fleet of battleships in the world, but it is very difficult to use them in action. For them the greatest danger comes from the air. Remember the *Bismark*!

With a certain amount of prescience Hitler realized that the day of the battleship was over—for all Navies. He had been deeply impressed that the Bismarck was crippled by torpedo-bombers and very much aware that the small ships of the German Navy—such as the powerful E-boats —were far more frequently in action than the big ones. The peak of success for major German warships occurred in March 1941 when the 'pocket battleship' *Scheer* and the battlecruisers *Scharnhorst* and *Gneisenau* sank or captured 17 British ships. In general, they provided the British Admiralty with a great deal of worry, but they never looked like being a war-winning weapon.

It was, in fact the U-boat that was the deadliest threat to Allied victory. The German U-boat commander, Admiral Donitz, believed that Britain would be forced to surrender if he sank 700,000 tons of shipping a month— probably an overestimate. As soon as the strategic situation turned in Germany's favour with the fall of

France, the U-boat aces began to make huge bags. In June 1940 they sank 284,000 tons and by October this had increased to 350,000 tons. When this was taken together with the efforts of the 'Kondors', mine-laying aircraft and surface warships it was obvious that the British were going to lose their struggle to survive.

This was the period that the German U-boat commanders later called the 'happy time'—when the British were so short of convoy escorts that they could only shepherd their charges as far as 15° west. After that, the U-boats cruising freely to 25° west from their new French bases sank their defenceless prey almost at will.

Below: Bismark, *the newest of Germany's capital ships, threatened to sever Britain's convoy lifeline. In a deadly game of hide-and-seek, the older ships of the Royal Navy scoured the northern waters for her, and eventually caught her. Here the* Bismark *engages the* 44,600 *ton* Hood, *an early victim of the battle, which went down with all but three of her crew.*

The winter brought the British some respite but, in the spring of 1941, the U-boats returned employing new 'wolf pack' techniques—homing in on a convoy in strength, and whittling it down by repeated night attacks. As the U-boats made these attacks on the surface, the asdic of the convoy escorts was rendered useless. In June, 310,000 tons of shipping was lost and the Germans began to express amazement that British sailors were not deterred from manning their ships—particularly the tankers which burned so fiercely. Hitler himself payed an approving tribute to his dogged enemy the next year. But the British fought with ingenuity as well as determination.

27 MARCH   **1942**

A patriotic fanaticism inspires Britain's airmen and sailors.

Submarines of the time could only make about 4 knots when submerged and needed to surface to recharge their batteries. A surface cruising speed of 12 knots meant that the U-boats normally proceeded to their stations submerged as little as possible. The RAF maintained patrols over the Bay of Biscay to try and catch and sink U-boats on the surface, or to delay them by forcing them to dive. Through 1941, passage across the Bay could only be carried out safely at night. At the same time, the Royal Navy increased the number of escort vessels available for convoy duty. It was also greatly assisted by the efforts of the Royal Canadian Navy and the rather less than neutral attitude of the US Navy—which provided escorts for American ships bound for Britain. This meant greater and continuous protection for convoys. Long-range aircraft supplied by lend-lease increased the arc of air cover over the Atlantic. On the debit side was the fact that Donitz had as many as 56 submarines operational by July 1941.

On balance, the help of the United States and the vigorous countermeasures brought the British back into the battle. Sinkings declined in the autumn, but when Hitler reflected on British skill in swift ship repair at the end of the year, he should have paused to consider that his enemies were driven by necessity. Shipping was very short, and the British people were tightening their belts in the face of real scarcity.

When America officially entered the war in December 1941, the effect was, paradoxically, for Allied shipping to be sunk in even greater quantity. Hitler had been keen not to antagonize the United States and give them a *casus belli;* German submarines had been forced into scrupulous observance of the conventions of American neutrality. Once this was over, the U-boats were freed to expand their operations further west—sinking an enormous tonnage of totally unprotected American coastal shipping. The Allies were only saved from even higher losses when Hitler autocratically ordered Donitz to send valuable U-boats to the defence of Norway—convinced that there would soon be an Allied counterstroke in the North.

22 JANUARY   **1942**

Norway is the zone of destiny.

Despite this diversion of force, the U-boats made 1942 a year of peak achievement. In both February and March they sank 500,000 tons, and this rose to 700,000 tons in June as the American admirals were slow to adopt the convoy system. This dreadful toll lessened slightly in July

but was up to well over 700,000 tons again in November.

The U-boat war was essentially a war of technology and, in late 1942, the Germans appeared to be winning it. They had over 300 operational submarines and they were introducing the new, large 'U-cruiser' of 1600 tons which had a range of 30,000 miles. On the other hand, the British had fitted the Leigh Light device to the patrolling RAF Sunderland aircraft which haunted the Bay of Biscay—ensuring that the U-boats now had no safe crossing by day or night. In October, the Germans moved one step ahead with their Metox receiver which gave warning of British radar probes and enabled the U-boats to take avoiding action.

1942 was a year of such success for the U-boat that Hitler was complacently noting the advantages of technological superiority. Even he was now able to see the relationship between military equipment and achievement —it was not all a question of morale—and it was dawning on him that a comparatively minor investment in U-boats saved him from facing a mass of military equipment that was, almost daily, being sent to the bottom. He was typically more concerned by British supplies to Russia on the notoriously dangerous Arctic convoys than on strangling British trade at its source in the open Atlantic. Despite the appalling cost, the Arctic convoys brought Russia 5000 tanks and over 7000 aircraft in 4,000,000 tons of cargo—an indication of the immense amounts of war material being shifted around the world in Allied hulls. Without the sinkings and disorganization caused by the U-boats, Germany would surely succumb before the sheer weight of Anglo-American armaments production.

Opposite: *U-47—commanded by Gunther Prien, Donitz's favourite commander—infiltrated the British home fleet's base at Scapa Flow on 13 October 1939, sinking the Royal Navy's battleship HMS* Royal Oak.

However, the vital lead in technology was snatched by the Allies in 1943. The Allies introduced new radar which defied detection by Metox. They also changed their code cypher which had been cracked and used by the Germans—although this was unknown at the time—and, as a reversal of positions, the Allies now had machinery to pinpoint a U-boat's position by its radio transmissions. Added to all this was the vast increase of available convoy escorts and of long-range air cover. In the Bay of Biscay, the U-boats tried to fight it out with the patrolling RAF. Although honours ended about even—with six U-boats sunk and six aircraft destroyed in May 1943—the aircraft were cheaper and easier to build and there were many more of them. In the Atlantic, the Allies no longer restricted themselves to driving U-boats off convoys but formed special groups of warships to hunt them to the death. From June to August 1943 only 58 Allied merchant ships were lost to U-boats, while 79 U-boats were destroyed in return.

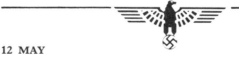

12 MAY   **1943**

There can be no question of a let-up in submarine warfare. The Atlantic is my first line of defence in the West.

When the tide turned against him, Donitz wished to withdraw his forces from the Atlantic until he had perfected new methods. With rare perceptiveness, Hitler forbade this. He was beginning to realize that the Battle of the Atlantic was being fought for the highest stakes of all. Yet, in the face of improved Allied techniques of sub-hunting, continuation of the struggle proved too much.

To make matters worse, Donitz was unable to extract any co-operation from the Luftwaffe. The deadliest antidote to the submarine was the aircraft, and Donitz begged Reichsmarshal Goering for some effort to give his U-boats air cover. The Luftwaffe was, however, a beaten service in the West. In any case, Hitler had no sympathy with using such German aircraft as could be deployed for protecting submarines. Whatever he had he wanted to use to smash British cities as a reprisal for the Allied bomber offensive. He even expressed reservations about using the Luftwaffe to mine British ports.

25 JULY   **1943**

In my opinion all this mining is useless. It gives no lift to our people and it does not affect those people over there either. There is no use now in talking about enemy ships being sunk—it does not impress the German people a bit.

By mid 1943 the Battle of the Atlantic was, to all intents and purposes, won by the Allies. The struggle continued right into 1944, but the U-boats kept suffering more heavily than Allied merchant ships. 1943 was the year in which the resources for invading the continent were ferried across the Atlantic to Britain so that, by the year's end, the strategic situation had changed. By then, Hitler was tacitly acknowledging that the struggle had shifted nearer to him: the U-boats were to be pulled back to combat the invasion rather than to contest the Atlantic, and their very bases were in danger from the air. By the end of May 1944, 70 U-boats were concentrated in the Bay of Biscay to combat the threatened landings and only three were in the Atlantic. During the last phase of the war, when the liberation of France had driven the U-boats back from their pens at Brest, Lorient and St Nazaire, they undertook little but prepared for a new offensive. New types of U-boat which were more than a match for the Allied techniques were produced, and in March 1945 the fleet reached peak strength with 463 submarines in service. The final victory of the Allied armies prevented the renewal of the U-boat menace and closed the chapter on one of the most vital battles of the war.

Left: *A rare picture of Donitz and Raeder together; with greater support from Hitler, their Navy might well have succeeded in winning the Battle of the Atlantic.*

BOMBER OFFENSIVE

THE BOMBER OFFENSIVE has been the subject of controversy and even shame among the victors of the war, and the unabashed use of terror bombing by the RAF High Command has since been regretted.

6 SEPTEMBER   **1942**

The British have no conception of chivalry in war. It is essential that we should give them as good as we get . . . the hanging of half a dozen British generals would shake them. They are realists, devoid of any scruple and cold as ice. It was the British who started air attacks. For four months we held our hand. The German is always restrained by moral scruples . . .

According to Hitler, the bombing was of British instigation and the British were a race of cold-blooded fiends to whom the ideas of pity or scruple were foreign. The answer was to descend to their level, which the Fuhrer could contemplate without too much distress, and start breaking all the conventions of war. Whenever he heard of a particularly violent RAF bomber attack, Hitler used to bay for revenge screaming that 'terror can only be broken by terror'. How his advisers prevented him from issuing orders for a general massacre of British prisoners will never be known.

Despite the Fuhrer's convictions about the naturally evil nature of the Briton, there can be little doubt that the indiscriminate bombing of civilians was begun by the Germans in both World Wars. In fact it was experience of this in World War I that led the British to steer clear of beginning such a bombardment—although the Germans happily accomplished the immolation of Warsaw in 1939. Following the raids of Gotha bombers on London in 1917-18, the British had become grossly over-impressed by the effect of such action on morale. They also had a brand new and independent military service in the Royal Air Force, and this naturally strove to promote its importance and guard its independence by stressing that the air weapon could bring victory in future wars without the assistance of ground troops. This meant that the British entered the war with a pro-bomber attitude, but with a bomber force that was greatly inferior to that built up by the Luftwaffe. The result was a certain caution—after all, if you believe that a bomber force is a war-winning weapon and that the enemy has a superiority in it, it is certain folly to begin a bombing campaign.

The Germans may have shared this unease or have been unconvinced of the strategic value of a long-term bombing campaign, for they were not quick to begin one. But they did realize the shock value of a concentrated assault on an enemy city. First Warsaw in 1939 and then Rotterdam in 1940 suffered a savage pounding which produced the required surrender. The effects of the Rotterdam bombing were much exaggerated but, instead of inspiring fear in Britain, they sparked off a resentful fury which diminished repugnance of reprisals by indiscriminate bombing. On 15 May, the day after the attack on Rotterdam, the RAF was instructed to attack German industrial targets. Unfortunately, 1939 had shown that day time raids were too dangerous, and Bomber Command was forced to undertake a night offensive without realizing that its navigational methods were so wildly inaccurate that this amounted to indiscriminate bombing.

For a while, the Germans observed the rules of bombardment—particularly as their cities escaped punishment during the Battle of Britain—and Bomber Command concentrated on invasion ports and shipping concentrations. The raids that could be made over Germany arguably produced the most important strategic gains of any bombing during the war—not because of the effect they had on German industry or morale but because of their effect on Hitler. They enraged the Fuhrer so much that he produced his famous promise to 'raze their cities to the ground' on 4 September 1940. Soon afterwards, the Blitz began lifting the pressure on Fighter Command but killing British civilians in large numbers and damaging their cities. This merciless attack served to absolve British consciences so that, when it was realized in mid-1941 that only one tenth of Bomber Command's machines found its way within five miles of the target, the British Air Staff were prepared to accept the concept of attacking German towns for the simple object of terrorization.

1941 brought some sort of lull in air operations in the West. The Germans had plenty for the Luftwaffe to do in Russia, and RAF Bomber Command was still woefully short of good heavy bombers. Added to this was the increasing effectiveness of the German defences—particularly the night fighters which made good use of a chain of defensive radar stations. All this blunted British ardour to incinerate German civilians, but there was never a complete disengagement.

Very early in 1942, Hitler sensed the wrath to come and began to make excuses for leaving such an imbalance of air forces in the West. Neither side had enough aircraft to undertake all it wished, he argued, so it was just one of the facts of modern war that you had to concentrate everything where it was needed most and, in the winter of 1941-2, the Luftwaffe's bombers were badly needed as transports for beleaguered German garrisons deep in Russia, such as 90,000 men of 16th Army at Demiansk.

On 14 February 1942, a directive to Bomber Command emphasised that bombing was to be 'focused on the morale of the enemy civil population'—terror was official. This unedifying attitude was compounded by depression and failure—Bomber Command was just about Britain's only offensive weapon, and it simply did not have the accuracy to be used against specific targets. At about the same time, Hitler made his own assessment of the value of bombing and the need for accuracy.

9 FEBRUARY 1942

Ten thousand bombs dropped on a city are not as effective as a single bomb aimed with certainty at a powerhouse or a water-works. The problem of bombardment should be considered logically.

For once, Hitler indulged in a fairly sober and reasoned analysis. He was an erratic man and his love of violence and drama had led him to order the 'razing ' of British cities and to decree that Moscow and Leningrad should be 'wiped off the face of the Earth', but he was capable of cooler and more logical thought. But, while everyone dwelt on the superior results which could be obtained by accuracy, RAF Bomber Command maintained that it could not be achieved.

The nub of the RAF bombing campaign in 1942 was the famous '1000-bomber raids'. Bomber Command's first-line strength in May 1942 was only 416 aircraft, but its new Commander-in-Chief, Air Marshal A.T. Harris, scraped together enough second-line and training squadrons to make the number up to 1046 bombers for a raid on Cologne on 30 May. The raid totally devastated 600 acres of that city. Similar sized assaults were made on Essen on 1 June and on Bremen on 26 June but, owing to cloudy conditions, less damage was inflicted. These three raids were the peak efforts of a year in which British bombers were in action as often as weather conditions allowed. Although this provided an unpleasant experience for the Germans, it was scarcely without cost for the British.

German searchlights and AA guns were directed by radar, but even their achievements were dwarfed by those of the night fighters. New radar sets were introduced during 1942 and the night fighters could be directed towards their prey with great precision by the *Wuerzburg Reise* radar before switching to the light, airborne *Lichtenstein* sets which took them to within sight of the chosen bomber. This specialized work was mostly carried out by two-seater German fighters and, by the end of 1942, the night fighter force numbered 389 aircraft (mostly ME 110s with a few Ju 88s and Do 217s). Against these machines, the RAF bombers were almost defenceless and casualties mounted alarmingly. In the raid on Bremen,

nearly five per cent of the bombers were brought down— a rate which, if sustained, meant that the average bomber crew could not expect to survive 20 missions.

While this struggle was going on, Hitler was far away from western Germany, which was absorbing the punishment, and concerned with organizing the Stalingrad disaster from his headquarters in the Ukraine and East Prussia. There is no doubt that news of it filtered through to him, but the Luftwaffe chiefs at least tried to minimise reports of damage—the Fuhrer could be an unpleasant prospect when upset by bad news. While things seemed to be going well in the East, Hitler's mood was fairly affable.

28 AUGUST 1942

Some German towns must be protected at all costs—Weimar, Nuremberg, Stuttgart. Factories can always be rebuilt but works of art are irreplaceable.

The assault on German cities had not then touched him on the raw and, where he did refer to the bombing, he showed that he had little knowledge of the problem— although German defences were very good, they could never be perfect.

By September the Fuhrer's attitude had changed and he was talking of hanging the captured captains of British merchant vessels in reprisal. These wild threats show that the bomber campaign was getting home, if only as a blow to Hitler's pride—it was certainly having little effect on German military potential. The Reich's armaments production increased about 50 per cent in 1942, while day and night fighter strength in the West grew very ominously indeed. For this, the RAF had lost 1291 bombers in a year. This prodigal sacrifice of bomber crews (who were hardly to blame that their lives were squandered in such a dubious enterprise) had produced very little effect on German morale.

12 DECEMBER 1942

It caused bad blood here at the beginning of the war and a few times thereafter, when, on the basis of Air Force reports it was announced that there had been very small damage when actually there had been great damage. It was especially shameless in Cologne . . . It is easier to bear the most brutal truth than an embellished picture which does not correspond to the truth.

Hitler himself recognized that the German people could bear the 'most brutal truth' if they were treated honestly by the authorities. It was strange that the British, who had stood up so well to aerial bombardment in 1940 and 1941, should imagine that it would break the Germans.

Despite all this, Bomber Command was growing ever stronger and was determined to give the Germans an even heavier pounding in 1943. It was to be joined in strength in this year by the 8th USAAF which was not committed to the indiscriminate methods of its British allies, but which was to make a genuine attempt to damage German war production and strategic supplies by accurate bombing. Unfortunately for the Americans, the only way to mount a massive but accurate bomber offensive in 1943 was to do it by day. They felt sure that well-armed bombers flying high in packed formation could fight off the German fighters—but this was not the case, and their daylight raids soon proved to be suicidal. Even when they used Thunderbolts to provide a fighter escort, their limited range meant that the bombers had to press on to most German targets unaided. If 1943 was disastrous for the Americans, they at least faced reality with more wisdom than the British, and made thorough preparations to contest the daylight skies of Europe in 1944 with a suitable long-range fighter.

For RAF Bomber Command, 1943 was a mixture of triumph and disaster. Navigation had been improving during 1942 with the introduction of the new aids *Oboe* and *H2S*, and raids were beginning to be preceded by the elite 'Pathfinder' force equipped with the Mosquito bomber, which could use *Oboe* because it flew at such a great height, and which marked the target for the following heavy bombers. In 1943 more and more of these bombers were the magnificent Lancasters with their huge range, payload and improved defences. All these factors helped in the 'Battle of The Ruhr' which Bomber Command undertook between March and July 1943 in a series of 43 major raids. Accuracy was much improved and damage to industrial plants as well as cities was severe, but the RAF still proved incapable of precision bombing on any scale. Nor could the British escape the grim harvest of the German defenders and they lost 872 planes in the campaign.

The Allied scientists did have a trick up their sleeve, however, which was used, for one brief interlude, to disorientate the German defences. On 24 July, 791 bombers began the 'Battle of Hamburg' when they approached that city dropping strips of metal foil to baffle the German radar. The new device was codenamed 'Window' and it caused pandemonium when it was first used. Hamburg was bombed literally round the clock by the RAF and the USAAF for a couple of days, and 17,000 bomber sorties were flown against the city between July and November. The effect on Hitler was electric.

Right: *A US bomb run over Berlin, 26 February 1945— destruction of the capital was now almost complete.*

**Terror can only be broken by terror.
That they attack airfields moves me little.
But if they smash our cities in the Ruhr...
I can only win the war if I destroy more of
the enemy's cities than he does of ours;
by teaching him the terrors of war.**

Hitler has often been accused of showing indifference to the suffering of the German people under the rain of bombs, but the ordeal of Hamburg seemed to give him real anguish. He had obviously been somewhat upset by the attacks on the Ruhr, but Hamburg was the last straw and he cried out for the only palliative he knew— revenge. He called on the Luftwaffe to destroy British cities, to give his enemies a taste of the horrors of war but, by this stage, the Luftwaffe bomber force was not equal to the task.

The casualties of British Bomber Command were as nothing compared with the Luftwaffe's loss of bomber aircraft during the winter of 1942-43. The prime cause of this was the special demands of the Russian campaign

and, most particularly, Hitler's orders that the surrounded Stalingrad armies should be supplied by air. The Wehrmacht simply could not function without air supply over the vast distances and tenuous communications of Russia, and the vital needs of soldiers did not stop when the weather was bad; so the Luftwaffe had to cope with bad weather and poor landing strips, as well as Russian flak and fighters. The three months of the Stalingrad airlift alone wrecked 1200 bomber and transport aircraft. With this heavy commitment in the East, the Luftwaffe could only make light raids on Britain.

However few their bombers, the Luftwaffe still kept enough fighters in the West to give them a winning hand during 1943. When the Americans ventured beyond the range of their fighter escort by day they were severely punished and the night fighters soon managed to find an antidote to 'Window'. A change of radio frequencies meant that the new German SN-2 radar sets operated outside the area jammed by 'Window', and the new homing devices *Naxos* and *Flensburg* used the British radar emissions themselves. The jamming device still made it difficult to spot an individual bomber, but the German night fighters could insert themselves into the bomber stream where a target soon came into view. This meant that after the first shock use of 'Window' in the 'Battle of Hamburg', RAF bomber losses began to grow again.

In November 1943, Bomber Command switched its main target from Hamburg to Berlin and concentrated on the German capital until March 1944. This did not mean that other German cities were left unmolested: raids were mounted on a number of other targets throughout 1943. However staunchly the German people bore this onslaught, there is evidence that it proved a strain to Hitler and many Nazi officials.

27 DECEMBER　　　　　　　　　　　　　　　　**1943**

The other day I had a failure in Kassel. You cannot say they have had it easy in Berlin or Hamburg; on the contrary . . . the man in Kassel just collapsed.

The Party *gauleiters* found themselves with the unwelcome job of coping with bomb damage, casualties and evacuees in their respective areas. Even Karl Kaufmann, the *gauleiter* of Hamburg, who was reckoned a tough character by Hitler, found it a bit much, and Goebbels recorded that he 'lost his nerve somewhat' after one raid on Hamburg.

Some boost to German morale was no doubt caused by the wreckage of so many British bombers which littered the Reich. The extra long haul to Berlin and back gave the night fighters additional chances, and the average loss rate soared above the horrific 5 per cent of previous

campaigns. On 30 March 1944, 94 bombers were lost and another 71 damaged out of 795 employed in an attack on Nuremberg. It was not realistic to ask bomber crews to take these sort of risks night after night for a vague objective and, in April, Air Marshal Harris was calling for night fighter cover which could not be provided. Luckily for Bomber Command, it was withdrawn from operations over Germany at about that time to destroy communications in France—in preparation for the Normandy landings. This served to disguise the fact that the RAF bomber offensive had been defeated by the Luftwaffe.

By that time, the Americans had returned to the fray with techniques which ensured complete Allied air superiority. During the bad weather of the winter of 1943-44 they had broken off their raids and provided themselves with adequate fighter cover. No amount of effort with the Thunderbolt and Lightning fighters really turned them into a match for all Luftwaffe day fighters or gave them sufficient range; but the scrambling of Allied technologies in the P51 Mustang produced a real war winner. When this American aircraft was equipped with a British engine and spark plugs, it not only had enough range to escort bombers as far as Germany's eastern borders, it was as good a fighter as either side possessed. When the 8th USAAF began operations again on 19 February 1944, a series of huge air battles took place against the defending Luftwaffe fighters and lasted for several weeks.

This American action was aimed primarily at aircraft factories and oil installations, although Berlin was included in March. The effect of the bombing was probably not that great, but the air battles broke the Luftwaffe. Within a few weeks the Mustangs gained control of the daytime skies of Germany and, instead of sticking to escorting their bombers, were able to roam far and wide seeking out German fighters. The Germans had long lost daytime control over northern France where the masses of shorter range British spitfires and Tempests had been operating in swarms since 1941. With the success of the Allied armies in liberating France, these superb British fighters could operate from bases near enough for them to join the Mustangs in the daytime skies over Germany. By the end of 1944, the Luftwaffe seemed to be smashed in everything but its night fighter operations and, in recognition of this, RAF Bomber Command was putting in a number of daylight raids.

This was the grim situation that faced Hitler when he turned his attention to the West in the autumn of 1944. Hitler was never foolish enough to dismiss the effect of air power and he realized that the colossal Allied superiority provided him with a problem. Despite every disadvantage, he managed to scrape together 1000 fighters and nearly 400 ground attack aircraft which were to deliver a surprise blow parallel to the unsuspected Panzer assault in the Ardennes. The idea was for these planes to deliver a crippling blow on the Allied airfields at first light and keep the Allied fighter bombers from harrassing the Panzers on their victorious drive through Belgium. If all went well, the Fuhrer reasoned, the enemy's short range fighters would be driven back from Germany's frontiers by his reconquests and this would give the Luftwaffe's latest aircraft types (which would include jets) a chance to take out the Mustangs. In the end, this winter air offensive was a disaster. Bad weather held the Luftwaffe back until 1 January 1945—when the Panzers had been stopped on the ground—and the results were simply not good enough. A lot of Allied aircraft were destroyed on the ground, but they could be quickly replaced, while some of the German fighter wings (*Jagdgeschwader*) had 30 per cent losses which could not be made up. In the West there were ten trained Allied pilots and any number of aircraft to any single German—that sort of disadvantage could not be reversed and only became worse as a result of the New Year's Day surprise attack.

In the final months of the war, the Allied bombing reached a crescendo which did finally destroy the German war effort. Until then the most significant efforts had been made against Axis oil installations which had produced

such an embarrassing shortage of fuel that the Luftwaffe had been forced to suspend training flights. German industry had struggled on because it had been carefully dispersed to elude the bombers, but the total Allied air superiority of 1945 brought collapse. This was the result of Allied concentration on communications targets: roads, railways, canals and bridges. Under these conditions, the war could not last much longer, and most Germans knew it. Unfortunately, Hitler was slow to concede defeat—even in the air war.

Just as Hitler kept directing phantom armies from his bunker, so he continued to plan for new aircraft types and, absurdly, to use an avenue through Berlin's Tiergarten Park as a runway for fighters. He refused to accept the bombs raining down on Berlin as much more than a temporary setback, until just before his suicide.

Below: *A German anti-aircraft company in action.*
Just prior to being withdrawn from operations over Germany, Bomber Command's losses were exceeding five per cent.

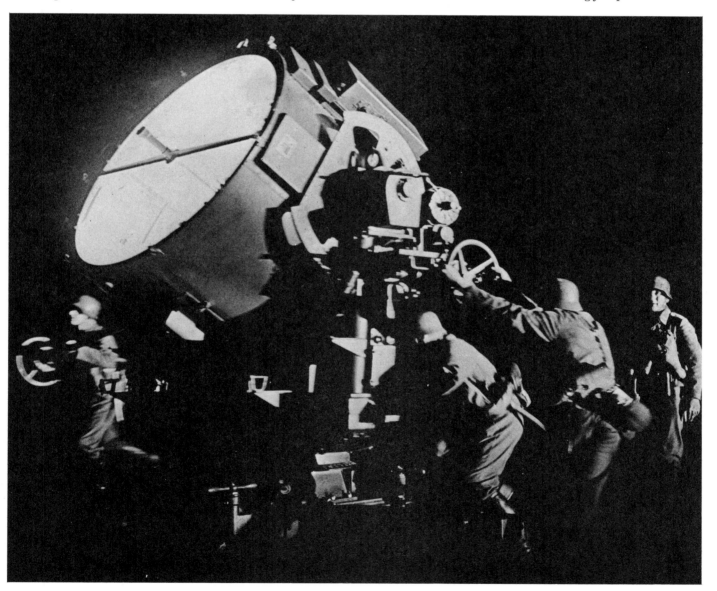

INDEX